LAST
THINGS
REVEALED

LAST THINGS REVEALED

Hope for Life and the Everafter

DR. JIM DIXON

Transforming lives through God's Word

Transforming lives through God's Word

Biblica provides God's Word to people through translation, publishing and Bible engagement in Africa, Asia Pacific, Europe, Latin American, Middle East, and North America. Through its worldwide reach, Biblica engages people with God's Word so that their lives are transformed through a relationship with Jesus Christ.

Biblica Publishing
We welcome your questions and comments.

1820 Jet Stream Drive, Colorado Springs, CO 80921 USA
www.Biblica.com

Last Things Revealed
ISBN-13: 978-1-60657-101-9

Copyright © 2011 by Dr. Jim Dixon

13 12 11 / 6 5 4 3 2 1

Published in 2011 by Biblica Publishing
All rights reserved. No part of this book may be reproduced in any form without permission in writing from the publisher, except in the case of brief quotations embodied in articles or reviews.

A catalog record for this book is available through the Library of Congress.

Printed in the United States of America

Contents

FOREWORD

There is much that I have come to admire about pastor and teacher Jim Dixon ever since my wife Leslie and I became part of Cherry Hills Community Church in Highlands Ranch, Colorado, in 2009.

First, I admire his biblical fidelity. Above all else, he strives to faithfully exegete the Word of God. Second, I've been impressed by his strong intellect, incredible depth of knowledge, and relentless pursuit of truth. Third, I've benefited from his relevant and warm teaching style. Fourth, I've appreciated his humility and willingness to admit the limits of how much we can know with certainty. And fifth, I've seen up close his sterling character, effective leadership, and wonderful sense of humor.

All of these fine qualities are reflected in this sound exploration of the end times, a topic that has confused and divided many Christians. In typical Dixon fashion, he carefully defines what we can know with confidence from the Bible, he delineates the different viewpoints on matters in dispute, and he offers his own perspective only where he can back it up with surety from Scripture.

This topic of the end times can create heated arguments among believers; indeed, I have friends who vigorously defend various theological positions. We can all agree to disagree on some of the specifics, but we ought to rally around those teachings that we can know for certain—the ones that come through loud and clear from the Bible. That's what Jim endeavors to do in this helpful and encouraging book.

If you're like many Christians who have only a murky understanding of the end times—and perhaps wrestle with fear about the future as a result—this book will bring clarity out of confusion and help you rest in the security of God's love and his plan for humankind. What's more, you'll walk away with relevant teaching that will change your life starting today.

I'm grateful for Jim's friendship, leadership of the church, consistently excellent preaching, and his encouragement in my life. After reading this book, I'm sure you're going to be thankful for his balanced and biblical approach to this daunting yet critically important topic.

Lee Strobel
Author, *The Case for Christ*

ACKNOWLEDGMENTS

The following people have provided the necessary reminders, urgings, gifts, and talents to get this book completed. Thank you,

Jim Shaffer—For faithful leadership in the publishing process

Blythe Daniel—For assisting Jim Shaffer throughout the entire project

Steve Rabey—For using your considerable editing and writing skills and for partnering with me

Lee Strobel—For your friendship and the foreward to this book

Dutch Franz—For encouraging me to write books

Barbara—For being my wife and partner in ministry. We are blessed.

Cherry Hills Community Church, staff, elders, and congregation . . . I am humbled and grateful to be your pastor and friend.

— 1 —

INTRODUCTION:

AN ANTIDOTE TO ANXIETY

The world did not end last year, but you'd never know it from viewing some of the popular end-of-the-world movies playing in theaters. *The Road,* based on the acclaimed Cormac McCarthy novel, follows an unnamed father and son on their desperate search of food and signs of civilization—in the barren wasteland of the United States, which, as the rest of the world, had been destroyed by an unknown catastrophe.

The film *2012,* released on a Friday the 13th in late 2009, portrays what would happen if ancient Mayan "prophecies" of the world ending on December 21, 2012, finally came true. According to *The Washington Post,* the movie's promotional campaign inadvertently scared many people: "Sony has set up a fake website for something called the Institute for Human Continuity—http://www.instituteforhumancontinuity.

org—that uses scientific-sounding language to detail the upcoming shredding, torching, and obliterating of the world from so many directions it makes your head spin."

And, *The Book of Eli* features Denzel Washington as a loner whose mission is to preserve the last remaining Bible in the world, nearly destroyed decades earlier by war.

Cultural critics struggled to explain these movies. One writer explored "cinema's apocalyptic obsession." Another wrote an article entitled "An End without End: Catastrophe Cinema in the Age of Crisis."

Throughout history, people have wondered how the world will end. These concerns have perhaps been amplified in recent years by the worldwide economic collapse, the rise of global terrorism, and the rapid cultural changes brought about by advances in technology, medicine, and the Internet.

But fears of the world's end are not new. In 1947, a group of atomic scientists created "the Doomsday Clock." On this symbolic clock, the closer the hands were to midnight, the closer we were to being blown to smithereens by an atomic bomb, so these scientists predicted. The clock was created during the Cold War, which pitted the United States against the then-Soviet Union. In 1947, the clock hands were set to seven minutes before midnight, which meant the scientists believed our world was on the verge of self-destruction. In 2010, the clock's hands were moved ahead to six minutes before midnight.

Everyday Apocalypse

My wife, Barb, and I came of age during the 1960s, a tumultuous decade that made many people feel the end was near. Those of us who lived in the '60s saw a president, other government officials, and social reformers such as Martin Luther King Jr. shot dead in their prime. We saw the growth of a large, youth countercultural movement that called into question many things the establishment assumed made life worth living.

As did many others, Barb attended lectures Hal Lindsey held at the University of California, Los Angeles. Lindsey's book *The Late Great Planet Earth* (1970) sold 30 million copies. It tapped into people's anxieties and even intensified them by asserting that the second coming of Christ would happen soon, probably no later than 1988.

More recently, the *Left Behind* novels, which altogether sold more than 50 million copies, fascinated many people. The *Left Behind* books do a good job showing us how one particular view of the end times might work out. But these books present only one view. That's important to remember. We shouldn't choose our position on any important issue based only on a series of novels.

Apocalyptic themes are explored not only in Christian books but also in mainstream novels. Jean Hegland's *Into the Forest* tells what happened when two girls try to grow up on their own after society had fallen apart around them. For some people, reading books or seeing movies about these issues is little more than entertainment. But for others, these only add to their worries about the future.

Questions about the End

How and when the world will end troubles all people, no matter what they believe or don't believe about God and his

Word. For Christians, questions and arguments about the end times revolve around a long list of variously interpreted Bible passages. These controversial passages discuss events that will happen to the human race and our planet in the future.

So, it was only natural that members of Cherry Hills Community Church—the Denver-area church where I've served as pastor for more than twenty-five years—raised questions about the end times following the attacks of September 11, 2001. Those events caused many Americans anxiety about a small but committed group of Muslims who were determined to bring our nation to its knees. The congregation wanted to understand what God had to say about the end of the world—and what they should do about it. In talking to people in our church, I made a shocking discovery: in all my years as pastor of Cherry Hills, I had never preached on these topics.

You may find that surprising, since some churches frequently focus on the end times. In fact, some preachers concentrate on these topics to the exclusion of other biblical matters. I think that's taking things too far. But we had the opposite problem; we had discussed it too little. I had not given these matters the attention they deserved. So, I determined to change that. After all, a significant number of Bible texts address these issues.

We scheduled far in advance a sermon series on the end times. I reviewed all the relevant passages and studied what leading biblical scholars have concluded. I also looked at some of the bestselling books on the subject. Then I preached a series of eight sermons called "The Last Things."

The response to this sermon series was more powerful than I could have anticipated. Many long-time members found new insights into their faith. Others who had never been to our church attended the series. Many of those came to faith in Christ when they learned more of what the Bible says about the end times.

The reaction was so strong we even scheduled a series of question-and-answer sessions, which allowed people to ask about some of the issues we did not have time to address in my sermons. The rarely discussed uncertainties and concerns of people had a chance to surface and be addressed. It was a wonderful time of spiritual growth and even healing for some who had grown fearful of the future.

When the series concluded, I was quite content to move on to the next sermon series on our schedule. But church members and leaders had another idea. They urged me not to pack up my notes and file them away. Instead, they wanted me to write a book that could help people outside the walls of our church make sense of these issues. With some 200,000 books published in the United States every year, I had to ask why we needed another one!

But they persuaded me that the way this topic had been handled in our church was unique and provided something Christians elsewhere needed to hear. Instead of promoting only one approach to controversial passages and ignoring the views held by other Christians, we gave all valid interpretations a fair hearing. And, instead of focusing on things that are marginal or merely frightening, we emphasized things at the core of Christian teaching about our hope for the future.

Now, years after people encouraged me to start this process, you hold that book in your hands. My prayer is that it will help you separate the wheat from the chaff in all the speculation about the end times.

God's Word: Our Antidote

Many people experience anxiety about the future. Some worry about the threats of terrorists and nuclear weapons. They wonder whether *this* battle or *that* weapon will bring about the end of the world. Will human beings blow themselves up, or will other forces end millennia of life on this blue-green planet? In a sense, questions such as these are at the heart of the Bible.

And, many people are confused about the end times. They may have an idea of what Hal Lindsey wrote in 1970 or what Nostradamus predicted centuries ago. But they are confused about what the *Bible* says. That's not surprising. Many Bible passages address these issues, but it's a challenge to interpret and harmonize them all.

In this book, I share with you some of what I've learned in my decades of studying, discussing, and teaching what the Bible says about "the Last Things." My primary goal is to reduce your confusion and anxiety by helping you unlock the teachings of God's Word. To achieve that goal takes an uncommon approach: we will look at the key arguments of a variety of interpretations to find those most in line with biblical teaching. In doing so, we'll emphasize our hope for the future.

I pray you'll learn several things.

First, I want you to grow in your understanding of the issues involved and in the Bible's core teachings on these matters.

Second, I want you to transcend any fear you may feel regarding end times and grow in your sense of peace about your relationship to God and his redemptive work in our world.

And third, I want you to grow confident in your faith and in your commitment to reach out to others with the love of God in the time we have left.

Agree to Disagree

Robert Gundry is a respected Bible scholar who taught at Westmont College in Santa Barbara, California, for more than forty years. He recently told me that publishers could not distribute his latest book on eschatology (study of the Last Things) to Christian bookstores in the United States because the book came to conclusions that some people reject. In his book, Robert did not promote anything out of the theological mainstream; he merely offered views on the end times that differed from the current majority views.

Episodes such as this worry me, because I think such theological censorship fails to serve the needs of thinking Christians who want to investigate differing interpretations of the Bible. A rigid approach results in the animosity that sometimes erupts among Christians who disagree. Even the most knowledgeable and committed Christians may hold opposing views on these complex issues. I believe we should treat differing opinions on these matters with respect. Christianity is about truth; it is also about love. In John 17, Jesus prayed that his disciples would be one.

> I will remain in the world no longer, but they are still in the world, and I am coming to you. Holy Father, protect them by the power of your name, the name you gave me, so that they may be one as we are one. While I was with them, I protected them and kept them safe by that name you gave me. None has been lost except the one doomed to destruction so that Scripture would be fulfilled. I am coming to you now, but I say these things while I am still in the world, so that they may have the full measure of my joy within them. I have given them your word and the world has hated them, for they are not of the world any more than I am of the world. My prayer is not that you take them out of the world but that you protect them from the evil one. They are not of the world, even as I am not of it. Sanctify them by the truth; your word is truth. As you sent me into the world, I have sent them into the world. For them I sanctify myself, that they too may be truly sanctified. My prayer is not for them alone. I pray also for those who will believe in me through their message, that all of them may be one, Father, just as you are in me and I am in you. May they also be in us that the world may believe that you have sent me. I have given them the glory that you gave me, that they may be one as we are one—I in them and you in me—so that

they may be brought to complete unity. Then the
world will know that you sent me and have loved
them even as you have loved me. (John 17:11–23
TNIV)

So far, that prayer has not been answered.

I hope that my teachings and writings focus on the important things and allow debate on the peripheral things. The fact that Christ will return to Earth to judge the world is an important doctrinal truth. The precise timing of his return is something on which we can disagree—without having to declare each other enemies of the faith.

In our world, I see many challenges that Christians could help solve. There are social problems and health issues that require all of us to hold hands and march into battle together. There are spiritual battles brought against us by Satan and his demonic forces. But if believers constantly bicker with one another, we will be too weak and too divided to stand together and do what we need to do as the hands and feet of Jesus in our day. If we start by shooting each other, the battle is lost before we begin.

Truth, but Not Exhaustive Truth

Some people want preachers, or authors, to pontificate and demand absolute loyalty to every word they teach. That's not my way. Nor is it the best approach in teaching people how to study the Bible. I'm not the only person to whom God gave a brain. He also gave one to you.

I want to present what the Bible says. In many cases, the testimony of the Bible is clear and straightforward. I'll point these out as we come across them in the following pages. But other passages are more complex. When it's difficult to determine what the Bible is teaching, when the biblical evidence is uncertain, I'll let you know and encourage you to make up your own mind.

In the end, you will at least have seen differing perspectives on the issues rather than me picking a perspective and telling you to believe it.

From Fear to Faith

Even though tough times are coming for our world, God is in charge. Confusion about the order and timing of events often leads to anxiety. And when people don't know what to believe, they also don't know what to do. That's why many pages of this book remind us that, even though we don't know everything about the end times, we can count on this: God is in charge, and all that happens will ultimately serve his purposes.

After 9/11, many people concluded the world is an unsafe place. They believe that we in the "Christian" West are at war with the "Muslim" Middle East, and that this conflict will bring about the end of the world. I guess anything's possible, but a careful reading of the Bible fails to uncover a conflict between the United States and the Middle East that leads to the end of the world.

Some people worry so much, they're convinced that the next vote for president, or for members of Congress, will determine whether the world ends sooner or later. God doesn't want us to be confused or troubled. If our relationship with him isn't what it ought to be, then he wants us to address that. But God doesn't want us to live in fear.

There are two kinds of fear: rational and irrational. If someone walks toward you with a gun and says, "I'm going to shoot you," fear would be a rational response. Hopefully that fear would stimulate your adrenaline so you could flee.

But if you get out of bed every morning, saying, "I know *this* will be the day someone shoots me," then that fear is probably irrational.

When it comes to the Last Things, many people are caught in irrational fears about things that may never happen the way they imagine. Some become so anxious they withdraw from others instead of reaching out to them in love, as God would have us do. They focus on stockpiling food in protective bunkers instead of breaking down barriers between themselves and other people.

That's particularly true today of Christians and Muslims. A primary goal in writing this book is to help believers live consistent with what the Bible teaches. That's why, in chapter three, we discuss Christianity and Islam. In that chapter, I urge people to find concrete ways to reach out to Muslims.

Yes, a very small group of radical Muslims seeks to kill us. But the Muslim men, women, and children who live near us, shop near us, and go to school near us are people created in the image of God. Our Father wants us to reach out to them, just as Jesus would. Unfounded anxiety keeps us from doing the things we ought to do, and if this book can help us move from a position of fear to a position of godly love for our neighbors, the time and effort spent researching and writing about these things will have been more than worth it.

Though we will look at some disturbing topics, such as hell and the tribulation, the Bible says, "The fruit of the Spirit is love, joy, peace, patience, kindness, goodness, faithfulness, gentleness and self-control. Against such things there is no law" (Galatians 5:22–23 TNIV). Nowhere does the Bible say the Spirit brings fear, anxiety, and paranoia. If we love God, then we should follow the example of David in Psalm 23: "Even though I walk through the valley of the shadow of death, I fear no evil; for thou art with me."

Satan and his demons operate the same way terrorists do. If we are afraid, they win. Fear is a rational response to some situations, but when it comes to the Last Things, God wants us to let go of fear and replace it with faith.

A Journey into Mystery

In the following chapters, we will stand outside of time today to look deeply into the future. We will travel with angels to peek into the glories of heaven. We will journey into hell to see scenes of incredible suffering. And we will watch from the sidelines as Christ defeats the powers of evil in the world's final battle.

I invite you to journey into the mystery of the Last Things. Not everything we see will be pleasing or clear-cut, but everything we encounter is essential to consider; otherwise, God would not have included these things in the Bible.

When we've completed this journey, I pray that you have a better understanding of the things to come, so that you make the most of your life and opportunities today.

— 2 —
HOW WILL IT ALL END?

For decades, Woody Allen has been making funny movies about serious subjects. He has also told his share of jokes about death, including: "It's not that I'm afraid to die. I just don't want to be there when it happens."

Isn't that how most of us feel about our own mortality? We know that someday we're going to die. In fact, death is one of life's few certainties. But dying is not something we talk about much in our culture. We try to keep thoughts of death at bay.

Many of us feel the same way about the end of the world. While some people are anxious about it, others give it little thought. Most of us, however, agree on one thing: we don't want to be there when it happens!

That's understandable. But I have an important question for you. If our world is coming to an end, doesn't it make sense to understand, as much as we can, how the end will occur, what it means to each of us, and what it will signify for the human race?

Life teaches us that everything comes to an end. I can prove this by reminding you of the "Macarena." Remember the hit song from 1995 that inspired a huge, but short-lived, dance craze? We may remember the song or the dance, but for many of us, this episode has been replaced in our brains by more recent or more important occurrences.

Pop-culture hits aren't the only things that end. The transience of life can be seen in our bodies, which grow, age, and ultimately pass away. Empires and nations are on top of the world one day, and little more than a chapter in history books the next. The same is true of the planets and galaxies that make up our cosmos. Even these billions of stars and star systems will end.

Many of us get our ideas about the end of the world from books, such as the *Left Behind* novels. Or from movies, such as *The Day After Tomorrow*. Or songs, such as "It's the End of the World As We Know It (And I Feel Fine)" by REM or the classic "Turn, Turn, Turn," which has been performed by everybody from the Byrds in the 1960s to Dolly Parton and Bruce Springsteen.

In fact, "Turn, Turn, Turn," written by folk musician Pete Seeger, is based on Solomon's sobering words in the Old Testament: "For everything there is a season, and a time for every matter under heaven: a time to be born, and a time to die" (Ecclesiastes 3:1–2).

When we hear the words *born* and *die,* most of us think of *human* life. But the Bible makes it clear that there is also a time for our *world* to be born and to die. The question is, are you ready? I hope this book will provide the wisdom and insight you need to say, "Yes!"

We begin by looking at the end of our world, as described by three sources: science fiction, science, and Holy Scripture. On this journey, I believe your eyes will be opened, your heart calmed, and some of your queasiness put to rest as you glimpse the amazing things God has in store.

The End, According to Science Fiction

One fall evening in 1938, millions of people were terrified by a radio broadcast reporting the world was ending. Many didn't realize they had heard a dramatic episode, produced by movie director Orson Welles, called "The War of the Worlds." Thinking they heard an actual news bulletin, people ran screaming from their homes in fear of Martian invaders.

More recently, the movie *The Day After Tomorrow* showed viewers what might happen if global warming were to melt the polar ice caps, elevating ocean levels around the world and unleashing a catastrophic flood in places such as New York City.

Most science fiction movies about the end of the world are a mix of fact and fancy. *Planet of the Apes,* the *Mad Max* films, and *Star Trek: First Contact* take something that's at least partially true or possible and combine this "science" with "fiction," which explores possible outcomes that may or may not ever happen.

We could spend the rest of this book examining the many ways science fiction and horror genres view the end of the world. In fact, one scholar has devoted an entire book to one moviemaker's take on the end. Kim Paffenroth, who has

LAST THINGS REVEALED

written scholarly tomes on Augustine, Dante, and Flannery
O'Connor, turned his attention to director George Romero
in *Gospel of the Living Dead: George Romero's Visions of Hell on
Earth* (Baylor University Press, 2006).

Paffenroth wrote that part of the reason for the perennial
popularity of zombie story lines—in classics such as *Dawn of
the Living Dead* and newer films such as *28 Weeks Later*—is
that we're fascinated by zombies, who "straddle the line between living and dead in a perverted version of the Christian
idea of bodily resurrection." (Find more on this at http://
en.wikipedia.org/wiki/End_of_the_world.)

What does science say about the end of the world? Some
of science's scenarios are as frightening as the made-up worlds
of science fiction.

The End, According to Science

There is no consensus among scientists as to how the world
will end. In one long-range scenario, thermonuclear reactions
at the sun's core will continue as normal for the next 4.5 billion years. But then, these reactions will destabilize, causing
the sun to expand. As it expands, the sun will generate sub-
stantially higher degrees of heat and light, turning everything
on Earth and throughout the solar system into one cosmic
crisp. The destruction in this long-range scenario would take
some 30 million years to run its course.

Some scientists look to the distant past to arrive at their
predictions for the future. In 1980, Nobel Prize-winning scientist Luis Alvarez studied geologic samples drilled from the
earth's core. Like the layers of sediment exposed in the Grand
Canyon, these core samples reveal events in the earth's past.

Alvarez grew puzzled when he found within the core samples unusually high amounts of iridium. This metallic element can be found on Earth but is one of the least-abundant elements in the earth's crust. Intrigued, Alvarez investigated. His research led him to a crater in the Yucatan Peninsula of Mexico, a 110-mile-diameter feature left by a large asteroid or comet striking the earth an estimated 65 million years ago. This collision not only left the iridium Alvarez was investigating, but it also blew 100 billion tons of sulfur dust into Earth's atmosphere, blocking out the sun's light for years and causing acid rain for decades, decimating all life on Earth (Leon Jaroff, "A Double Whammy?," TIME, November 6, 2003).

Alvarez isn't the only scientist exploring cosmic collisions. Scientists have found some two hundred craters on Earth, indicating how many times our planet has been hit by asteroids or comets. Most scientists believe that collisions like those in Earth's past will again happen in the future. And, perhaps, one of these would block out the sun and once again wipe out all life on Earth.

Meanwhile, astronomers are investigating other ways our world might end. In one scenario, a nearby star turns into a supernova, depleting our planet's ozone layer to destroy every living thing. Or, perhaps our planet could be destroyed by a slight shift in the earth's axis, which could bring about severe climactic changes that usher in a new global ice age.

If it seems as if scientists are pessimists, they're not. It's just that the survival of our planet and everything living on it depend on countless numbers of things working just right. Any deviation of even one of these precise balances could have catastrophic results.

Since science provides so many differing views of the end, is there a reliable source we can consult?

The End, According to the Bible

The Bible is not a science textbook, but it *is* a unique source of insight into how life began, how it will end, and how we should live our lives in the meantime. The chapters in this book examine some of the many "end time" lessons presented in the Bible.

One of these lessons is about "the great tribulation." Jesus taught about this period in a talk with his disciples before his crucifixion. Each of the three synoptic Gospels contains this teaching: Matthew 24:3–31, Mark 13:3–37, and Luke 21:5–36. In these passages, Jesus says the earth will experience tribulation "such as has not occurred since the beginning of the world until now, nor ever shall" (Matthew 24:21 NASB). Further details about this disaster can be found in Revelation, the final book of the Bible, which prophesies the destruction of one-third to two-thirds of Earth's air, soil, and water.

Over the years, Christians have discussed and debated which predictions made in the Bible, if any, have already happened. An event in 1948 grabbed the attention of Bible students and prophecy buffs around the world.

Many passages in the Bible say that in the last days Israel will be reborn as a nation and the Jewish people returned to their homeland. For centuries, Bible scholars thought such a development would be impossible in the Middle East. But many doubters became believers when the modern nation of Israel was established in 1948.

Mis-Counting the Days

According to Hal Lindsey's *The Late Great Planet Earth*, this event started the "countdown" toward the return of Christ. Lindsey, who wrote his book in 1970, predicted that Christ would return to Earth no later than 1988. Lindsey was wrong about his end-time predictions, but he wasn't the first to make such a mistake. Human history is rife with people who wrongly read the signs of the times.

Montanus was a charismatic convert to Christianity who lived in the second century after Christ. He taught that Christ would return soon; his committed followers believed him and left their mundane concerns behind, such as work and families, to await the coming of the New Jerusalem. After the death of Montanus, the movement's followers were excommunicated from the church and became an underground movement.

Three centuries later, as the Goths attacked Rome, a theologian named Pelagius announced the imminent end of the world and the return of Christ. Predictions of the end of the world accompanied the eruption of the volcano Vesuvius in 991. Further predictions were made as the calendar approached the year 1000. Many said the new millennium would be the *final* millennium of human history. Similar predictions were made as the calendar approached the year 2000. Remember Y2K (Year 2000)? It's a safe bet that history will repeat itself in the year Y3K.

Around the year 1191, Joachim of Fiore, an Italian monk, predicted the world would end in 1260. He also persuaded the king of England, Richard the Lion-Hearted, that joining forces with Christians fighting in the Crusades against Muslims would help usher in the final days.

In 1495, three years after Christopher Columbus arrived in the New World, a fiery Italian preacher named Savonarola set a date for the end of the world. After the uneventful date passed, fewer people turned out to listen to Savonarola's sermons. Less than a decade later, Columbus himself wrote a little-known book called *The Book of Prophecies*. One prophecy called for Jesus Christ to return in December 1656.

Centuries later, William Miller said Christ would return on October 22, 1844. Thousands of his followers, known as Millerites, quit their jobs, sold their houses, and waited for Jesus to arrive. When no such thing happened, the Millerites regrouped and founded the Seventh-day Adventist Church.

Nobody Knows

If these examples fail to prove how risky it is to predict the date of Christ's return, perhaps Christ's own words might convince you.

> But of that day and hour no one knows, not even the angels of heaven, nor the Son, but the Father alone. For the coming of the Son of Man will be just like the days of Noah. For as in those days which were before the flood they were eating and drinking, they were marrying and giving in marriage, until the day that Noah entered the ark, and they did not understand until the flood came and took them all away, so shall the coming of the Son of Man be. Then there shall be two men in the field; one will be taken, and one will be left. Two women will be grinding at the mill; one

will be taken, and one will be left. Therefore be
on the alert, for you do not know which day your
Lord is coming. (Matthew 24:36–42 NASB)

After Christ's death and resurrection, Paul needed to
remind Christians in Thessalonica of Jesus' words. Some of
these believers had left their jobs to await Jesus' return. But
Paul told them to get back to work. "But concerning the times
and the seasons, brethren, you have no need that I should
write to you. For you yourselves know perfectly that the day
of the Lord so comes as a thief in the night" (1 Thessalonians
5:1–2 NKJV).

Everybody who has ever studied the Last Things knows
that these verses tell us to avoid setting specific dates, though
that hasn't stopped some from writing books in which they
reject this advice. One of the most famous of these books was
Edgar C. Whisenant's *88 Reasons Why the Rapture Could Be in
1988,* which predicted the rapture would occur in September
of that year.

Some people spend too much time worrying about the
when. In this book, we focus on the *how* and the *why* so that
we will be at peace about the future. In the meantime, we can
focus on the two things Jesus told us are the most important
commandments of all.

But when the Pharisees heard that He had put the
Sadducees to silence, they gathered themselves
together. And one of them, a lawyer, asked Him
a question, testing Him, "Teacher, which is the
great commandment in the Law?" And He said
to him, "'You shall love the LORD your God with
all your heart, and with all your soul, and with

all your mind.' This is the great and foremost commandment. And a second is like it, 'You shall love your neighbor as yourself.' On these two commandments depend the whole Law and the Prophets." (Matthew 22:34–40 NASB)

In the Meantime

Christ may come back tomorrow, or next year, but there's no way to predict the time of his return with certainty. The best thing we can do, therefore, is figure out how to live our lives in the meantime.

That doesn't mean we forget the fact that the end is coming some day, both for us and for our world. Some people don't even like to whisper the word *death*. Yet only when we acknowledge that we will die, can we better approach the task of living.

There are two groups of people with unrealistic and unhealthy views of the future. One group is perpetually worried; they believe that the world will grow increasingly worse until it all goes, literally, to hell. The other group isn't worried at all. They view life as a party that will never end. Both of these approaches are illusions that prevent us from seeing the reality of our world and developing a realistic strategy for living in it.

Do Not Be Afraid

The Bible introduces us to many men and women who struck the proper balance. The apostle John was one willing to acknowledge his own mortality. He had walked and worked alongside Jesus. He saw Jesus crucified and celebrated his resurrection. Then he became a leader in the early Christian church. His tireless work for the faith in an antagonistic, pagan culture resulted in recurring persecution and, as an old man, his eventual banishment to the island of Patmos.

Today, we think of Patmos as a lovely Greek island. But in John's day, it was a place of exile, where the Roman government sent some of its worst prisoners. We believe that John lived on Patmos for about eighteen months. Sometime around the year 95, an amazing thing happened to John: Jesus appeared to him in a vision and showed him how the world would end. John wrote down most of what he saw, and those words became the Bible's book of Revelation.

Some people read Revelation and come away with frightening pictures of demons, death, and destruction. But for me, because of Jesus' words in the first chapter, Revelation is calming and reassuring. "Fear not, I am the first and the last, and the living one. I died, and behold I am alive forevermore" (Revelation 1:17–18 ESV).

Plenty of people find in Revelation things to fear. I've also wrestled with fear many times. But I always go back to those powerful words of Jesus: "Fear not." I hope you hear those words echoing from every page that follows.

A few years ago, Michael Stipe of REM sang these interesting words: "It's the end of the world as we know it (and I feel fine)." I don't know if he was being serious or sardonic. But there's no doubt about Jesus' words to the apostle John; they are words of hope, both for this life and the next, words we need to hear today.

With Jesus' words as our guide, perhaps the mysteries of the last days needn't fill us with fear.

"Fear not, I am the first and the last, and the living one."

— 3 —

FROM BROTHERS TO COMBATANTS:

ISAAC AND ISHMAEL. ISRAEL AND ISLAM

You can hardly turn on a television or radio, read a newspaper or magazine, or surf the Internet these days without coming across a news story about tensions between Israel—which was created as a national home for Jews after the Holocaust—and the predominantly Islamic nations of the Middle East.

Conflict between these two groups spans centuries, though few understand the deep spiritual issues that lie at the heart of this strife. Fewer still can foresee the important role these hostilities will play in the Last Things described in the Old and New Testaments. I believe these conflicts will continue to be a source of what the Bible calls "wars and rumors of wars" until it brings about the final battle—Armageddon, which will signal the beginning of the end of the world as we know it.

To understand both the historical causes and the ultimate outcomes of this ancient conflict between followers of these faiths, we must travel to a place called the Tomb of the Patriarchs.

A Troubled Tomb

The Tomb of the Patriarchs—also known as the Cave of Machpelah—is an historic site located in the West Bank town of Hebron, a short distance from Jerusalem. It is known as the Tomb of the Patriarchs because of the people buried there, including Abraham, Isaac, and Ishmael; Abraham's wife Sarah; Isaac's wife, Rebekah; and Leah, the wife of Jacob. A sacred site for thousands of years, one of the earliest references to it is found in the book of Genesis.

> These are the days of the years of Abraham's life, 175 years. Abraham breathed his last and died in a good old age, an old man and full of years, and was gathered to his people. Isaac and Ishmael his sons buried him in the cave of Machpelah, in the field of Ephron the son of Zohar the Hittite, east of Mamre, the field that Abraham purchased from the Hittites. There Abraham was buried, with Sarah his wife. (Genesis 25:7–10 ESV)

Abraham is referred to as a "patriarch" because he fathered many important descendants and multiple nations and creeds. From his seed came Moses, the Jewish religion, Jesus Christ, and the Christian faith. What some don't realize is that from the seed of Abraham also came Mohammed and the religion of Islam. Judaism and Islam came, respectively, through the descendants of Abraham's two sons, Isaac and Ishmael.

Some see Abraham's family as a classic dysfunctional family. Isaac and Ishmael were born into this dysfunction. Ishmael, fourteen years older than Isaac, was the son of Abraham through Hagar, the Egyptian maid of Sarah, Abraham's wife. Isaac was the son of Abraham through Sarah. A lifetime of animosity defined the relationship between Isaac and Ishmael. Even today, conflict between descendants of these brothers ripples around the world.

Though Isaac and Ishmael experienced much tension and conflict, like children everywhere, they stood side-by-side when their father died, sharing a common grief and a common love for Abraham. They were together that day at the Cave of Machpelah in Mamre—present-day Hebron—to bury their father.

But the calm between Isaac and Ishmael was only temporary. In time, tensions between the half-brothers would grow to global proportions.

For centuries, Jews guarded the Cave of Machpelah. But, after the birth of Islam in the seventh century and its increased power in the Middle East in the following centuries, the cave became a Muslim shrine. Today, a Muslim mosque stands tall above the cave.

Many things changed in 1967 with the Arab-Israeli War. Since then, the nation of Israel has occupied the West Bank, including Hebron and the Tomb of the Patriarchs—further troubling the relationship between Jews and Muslims.

On March 2, 1994, numerous Muslims—descendants of Ishmael—gathered at the Cave of Machpelah for a memorial.

On the same day, Berak Goldstein—a Jewish descendant of Isaac—visited the cave. Goldstein, however, did not intend to honor the dead. Instead, he had planned to cause death and mayhem. Reaching inside his coat, he grabbed the automatic weapon concealed there and began firing off shots, murdering forty-eight Arab Muslims—forty-eight descendants of Ishmael—before he was killed.

The following week, Jerusalem was the site of two memorial services. At the Jewish service, Rabbi Jachof Perin made this infamous statement: "One million Arabs are not equal in value to a single Jewish fingernail." At the Muslim service, PLO leader Kahil Aziz was equally incendiary, saying, "God Allah. Help us to murder every single Jew one-by-one until they are eradicated from the face of the earth."

Tensions between Jews and Muslims have not calmed since and, in fact, are as bad today as they've ever been. This conflict is a continuing source of war, death, and destruction in many nations around the world.

Of course, conflict isn't the case for all Jews and all Muslims. In fact, steps have been made in recent years to create avenues for interfaith dialogue and communication between members of these groups. Some Jews and Muslims have developed strong and lasting bonds of friendship.

On the other hand, there are people on the angry, radical fringes of both Judaism and Islam who feel nothing but hatred for people of other faiths. I believe this hatred and hostility will drive the world to a war unlike any the world has ever seen. The ultimate outcome of this ancient conflict will signal the consummation of human history.

For that story, we turn away from ancient history and current events to a fascinating passage in the final book of the Bible.

The War to End All Wars

The guns of battle were still sounding during World War I when commentators began calling it the "war to end all wars." People felt certain that no nation would ever want to subject its young men to the senseless and massive carnage experienced in the trenches of what was also known as the Great War. But as we know, this optimism was misplaced. World War II was even more destructive and murderous than World War I. And the decades since have shown no lack of global conflict.

But people who read the Bible know there will be a war to truly end all wars. Armageddon is the name the Bible gives to the final war of human history, described in the book of Revelation.

> And I saw, issuing from the mouth of the dragon and from the mouth of the beast and from the mouth of the false prophet, three foul spirits like frogs; for they are demonic spirits, performing signs, who go abroad to the kings of the whole world, to assemble them for battle on the great day of God the Almighty. ("Lo, I am coming like a thief! Blessed is he who is awake, keeping his garments that he may not go naked and be seen exposed!") And they assembled them at the place which is called in Hebrew Armageddon. (Revelation 16:13–16)

This is the only passage in the Bible where the word *Armageddon* is used, though the concept of a culminating battle between good and evil is also found in Old Testament passages such as Zechariah 14 and Ezekiel 38–39.

Numerous passages in Revelation point out that Armageddon will be fueled by Satan. In fact, the "foul spirits" mentioned in the passage above are actually evil or demonic spirits that will perform signs and wonders and will assemble all the kings of the world for battle on this fateful day. In other words, Armageddon will be driven by demonic hatred.

People say that, today, Christians are the ones on the receiving end of persecution and hatred. But Jews have been hated and persecuted around the world for centuries. In the 1940s, the Holocaust revealed the depths of that hatred. Inspired by demonic spirits, the Holocaust led to the systematic murder of an estimated 6 million Jews. Comparatively, the persecution Jews experience today is less severe; but, as we hear in the news, it still occurs all too frequently. The hatred unleashed toward Jews in the twentieth century provides a foretaste of this demonic hatred that will overflow all bounds and lead to the end of the world.

In the end times, demonic spirits will go forth causing even greater depths of hatred toward Israel. In time, this hatred will lead nations to rise up against Israel and the city of Jerusalem.

The word *Armageddon* comes from the Hebrew words *har,* meaning "mountains," and *Megiddo,* referring to the ancient city of Megiddo that was located in the Plain of Megiddo, also known as the Valley of Jezreel. The region of Megiddo has already been made famous for the many wars fought there throughout history. Judges 5 records the armies of Israel defeating the armies of Sisera at Megiddo. In 2 Kings 23 and 2 Chronicles 35, the armies of Pharaoh put down King Josiah, king of Judah, at Megiddo.

Because much of the book of Revelation is symbolic, some scholars are unsure if the final battle of Armageddon will be fought literally within the physical locale of Megiddo. I believe it will begin there before spreading around the world. Regardless of how you interpret the reference to Megiddo, the focus of the last global battle of human history is clear—hatred of Israel.

Ezekiel 38 and 39 say that, at the end of time, the nations of Gog and Magog (or "Gog, of the land of Magog") will come against Israel. There is much speculation as to the identity of these nations. In Ezekiel's day, Gog and Magog would have been associated with Persia, Cush, Put, Gomer, and Togarmish. These ancient nations are no more, but the lands they inhabited are, today, largely Arabic and Muslim.

In recent decades, prophecy buffs felt certain that these terms referred to Russia, the former Soviet Union. But other scholars have long argued that the words *Gog* and *Magog* refer to the Arabic nations that surround Israel. That was also the conclusion of Martin Luther, the pioneer of the Protestant Reformation, who wrote a booklet about Armageddon, saying that Gog and Magog were the "Mohammedan" (or Muslim) kingdoms surrounding Israel.

Overall, I think Luther got it right. The battle of Armageddon prophesied in the book of Revelation will see the Muslim nations rising up against Israel—in the war to end all wars.

If so, what does that mean for us today?

A Blessing to Isaac and Ishmael

Just hearing about Armageddon makes people worry. When some of these folks open the book of Revelation, they immediately begin plans to build underground bomb shelters that are stocked full of food and water. They mistakenly believe that they'll be able to separate themselves from the rest of suffering humanity by hunkering down and hiding out until things calm down.

But God doesn't want us to sit and wait. And the wait might be longer than we think. After all, each generation since the time of Christ has thought *theirs* is the one that will witness the end of the age. But Jesus said *no one* knows the hour or day of his return. We can, however, know what God wants us to do in the meantime. He wants us to love him and to love our neighbors. He wants us to be ambassadors of his love to our world.

If you continue reading the Genesis story of Isaac and Ishmael, you'll see that God gave a blessing to both sons of Abraham. God not only pronounced a blessing on Isaac and his descendants but God also pronounced a blessing on Ishmael and his descendants. Each son would become the father of a great people.

Likewise, we should bless both the descendants of Isaac and the descendants of Ishmael. We already work on the first half by praying for Israel and loving the Jews. But what about Islamic people? God wants us to bless them, too. At the end of this chapter, I suggest some practical ways we can do so.

God loves everybody. As followers of his Son, we must translate his love into our action. Instead of giving in to fear and hate, as so many people do today, we need to serve the Prince of Peace in *the ministry of reconciliation,* as described by Paul.

> For the love of Christ controls us, because we have concluded this: that one has died for all, therefore all have died; and he died for all, that those who live might no longer live for themselves but for him who for their sake died and was raised. From now on, therefore, we regard no one according to the flesh. Even though we once regarded Christ according to the flesh, we regard him thus no longer. Therefore, if anyone is in Christ, he is a new creation. The old has passed away; behold, the new has come. All this is from God, who through Christ reconciled us to himself and gave us the ministry of reconciliation; that is, in Christ God was reconciling the world to himself, not counting their trespasses against them, and entrusting to us the message of reconciliation. Therefore, we are ambassadors for Christ, God making his appeal through us. We implore you on behalf of Christ, be reconciled to God. For our sake he made him to be sin who knew no sin, so that in him we might become the righteousness of God. (2 Corinthians 5:14–21 ESV)

What does this mean for us today? For one thing, it means we take the gospel of Jesus Christ to the world—not as intimidating crusaders who enforce faith with the point of a sword, but as humble servants who offer to the world God's merciful grace. We are ambassadors of God's forgiveness. And the ministry of reconciliation requires that we not count peoples' trespasses against them. That includes Jews, and it includes Muslims.

In Judaism and in Islam, there is great respect for the *power* and the *justice* of God. But disciples of both Judaism and Islam struggle to understand the *love* and the *mercy* of God. We can help them grasp God's forgiveness, but only if we're willing to love and serve them.

That's not easy. Some reading these words may not be ready to forgive Muslims. Some may even hate Muslims. That's sad, because God is love, and he commands us to love our neighbor as ourselves. Here's what Jesus says in the gospel of Mark.

> And one of the scribes came up and heard them disputing with one another, and seeing that he answered them well, asked him, "Which commandment is the first of all?" Jesus answered, "The most important is, 'Hear, O Israel: The Lord our God, the Lord is one; and you shall love the Lord your God with all your heart and with all your soul and with all your mind and with all your strength.' The second is this: 'You shall love your neighbor as yourself.' There is no other commandment greater than these." And the scribe said to him, "You are right, Teacher. You have truly said that he is one, and there is no other besides him. And to love him with all

the heart and with all the understanding and
with all the strength, and to love one's neighbor
as oneself, is much more than all whole burnt
offerings and sacrifices." And when Jesus saw that
he answered wisely, he said to him, "You are not
far from the kingdom of God." And after that no
one dared to ask him any more questions. (Mark
12:28–34 ESV)

God hates *evil*, it's true. But he always loves *people*. I
hope you're willing to love people, too, including Muslims.
Nevertheless, loving and forgiving will not be easy for
everyone.

Nearly three thousand people lost their lives in the 9/11
attacks on the Twin Towers of the World Trade Center,
the Pentagon, and a passenger jetliner in the sky over rural
Pennsylvania. The men behind these attacks praised Allah as
they took themselves and thousands of others to their early
death. All who lost a loved one in these tragedies may find it
difficult to forgive and love Muslims.

Thousands more men and women have lost their lives or
have been injured in the fighting in Iraq and Afghanistan. I
won't debate these conflicts here. But, those who have suffered from these wars may also find it difficult to forgive and
love Muslims.

Other people may have other reasons not to forgive and
love, reasons they consider valid. But God's command to us
remains. When Jesus came to our planet, he did so because
"God so loved the world" (John 3:16)—the whole world, not
just part of it.

Love does not mean we are blind. It does not mean we ignore the fact that a radical fringe of Islam seeks to destroy all Jews and all Americans and is willing to drive the world to the brink of disaster in the course of pursuing that goal. Love does not mean we close our eyes to the injustices committed by groups such as Hamas, Hezbollah, and Al Qaeda. Love does not mean we ignore passages in the Koran that sound a call to arms against "infidels"—which means us (non-Muslims)!

But love *does* require us to acknowledge that most Muslims are good people trying to do the best they can. They're trying to be dads and moms, husbands and wives, sisters and brothers, workers and managers. They're doing the best they can to live life and submit themselves to Allah. The meaning of the term *Islam* is "submission."

Hate-filled Muslims on the radical fringe are not the norm. God loves Muslims. God loves all people. And he wants us to do the same.

Love in Action

A concept is little more than a thought unless you convert it into an action. We may *say* we buy into the concept of "loving everyone," but unless we translate our words into action, they remain just a thought. Let me explain.

A half-century ago, pollsters went door-to-door in the Deep South asking people's opinions on race. Early on, the pollsters asked, "Do you believe that all people are created equal?" A large number of southerners said, "Yes." But a later question wasn't as easy to answer. The pollsters asked, "Are blacks equal to whites?" Many white southerners in the 1950s and 1960s had trouble answering that question with a "Yes."

Is your love for other people qualified? Do you love some people but not others? And specifically, do you have trouble loving Muslims? Here's how we worked through some of these issues in our church.

At the time we were discussing Islam in our church, the devastating 2004 tsunami killed an estimated 230,000 people in fourteen countries—167,000 in Indonesia alone. Many people don't realize it, but the most populous Muslim country in the world is not Saudi Arabia or Iran. It's Indonesia.

After the tsunami hit, we encouraged our people to help care for Muslim families who had suffered through this tragedy. Some members made charitable donations they would not otherwise have made. Some even traveled to Indonesia with relief and development organizations to lend a hand. These are examples of putting love into action.

You may say, "That's great, but what can I do?" You don't need to wait for a tragedy to strike. Is there a Muslim family in your neighborhood? Then do something simple such as saying hello to them. Even better, practice the virtue of hospitality by asking them to dinner.

Maybe you don't know any Muslims. That's okay. If you're in a small group, Bible study, or home group, add to your group's prayer list the Muslims living in your community. Some people use the *30-Days Muslim Prayer Guide* materials to help them pray in a more focused and knowledgeable manner (http://www.30daysprayer.com).

Or, if you want to take the initiative to meet local Muslims, contact your local mosque. Most mid-sized cities in the United States have a mosque, though they don't look like the large buildings we see in the news. Many are small, humble spaces in storefronts or office buildings. You can locate a mosque in your area by looking in the yellow pages under "Islamic Society."

One important thing you can do is study. Many people are fearful of Muslims because they know nothing about them. They know only 9/11 and the Iraq and Afghanistan wars. But these events don't tell us much about the average Muslim man and woman. The following list of resources is designed to help Christians understand Muslims.

Books from Christian publishers and organizations
- Shirin Taber. *Muslims Next Door: Uncovering Myths and Creating Friendships* (Zondervan, 2004).
- William P. Campbell. *The Qur'an and the Bible: In the Light of History and Science* (Middle East Resources, 2002).
- Edward J. Hoskins. *A Muslim's Heart: What Every Christian Needs to Know to Share Christ with Muslims* (Dawson Media, 2003).
- Don McCurry. *Healing the Broken Family of Abraham: New Life for Muslims* (Ministries to Muslims, 2001).
- Keith E. Swartley. *Encountering the World of Islam* (Authentic, 2005).

Other recommended books
- Lawrence Wright. *The Looming Tower: Al-Qaeda and the Road to 9/11* (Vintage, 2006). This Pulitzer Prize-winning book provides a detailed look at the rise of anti-Jewish and anti-American Islamist terrorist movements.

- Karen Armstrong. *Muhammad: A Biography of the Prophet* (HarperSanFrancisco, 1993). This is an accessible study by the British scholar, but some critics feel Armstrong is too positive.
- Robert Spencer. *The Truth about Muhammad: Founder of the World's Most Intolerant Religion* (Regnery, 2006). This is a more critical book than Armstrong's biography.

General information websites
- www.answering-islam.org
- www.embracethetruth.org
- www.shoebat.org
- www.americancongressfortruth.org
- www.joelrosenberg.com

Classes and Events
I also encourage you to look for classes in your area that can help you understand Islam and learn ways other Christians are reaching out. Is there a church, ministry, or mission organization in your area that holds classes on Islam? Look around; you'll be surprised what you find and what you learn.

The tensions and animosities that spring from the two different paths taken by Isaac and Ishmael's descendants are having a destructive effect throughout our world. There's no way for us to end this conflict overnight. And nothing we can do will delay God's plans for Armageddon.

In the meantime, God wants us to do everything we can to love him and to love our neighbors, even our Muslim neighbors. Are you willing to join me in this important task?

— 4 —
TIMES OF TROUBLE
AND TRIBULATION

In the movie *Armageddon,* a meteor speeds toward Earth, threatening every living thing on the planet. Narrator Charlton Heston gives viewers the following introduction: "This is the Earth, at a time when the dinosaurs roamed a lush and fertile planet. A piece of rock just six miles wide changed all that. It hit with the force of 10,000 nuclear weapons. A trillion tons of dirt and rock hurtled into the atmosphere, creating a suffocating blanket of dust the sun was powerless to penetrate for a thousand years. It happened before. It will happen again. It's just a question of when."

Moviemakers love apocalyptic storylines because they offer so many possibilities for special effects. Good movies need dramatic tension, and nothing creates tension more than the end of the world. And, according to the movies, the end happens only with plenty of fireballs, explosions, and chaos. It makes for exciting cinema.

Writers, too, for centuries have explored the final chapter of human life on Earth. In his poem "The Hollow Men," the acclaimed British poet T. S. Eliot described the issue this way: "This is the way the world ends, not with a bang but a whimper."

Our fears and fascinations about the end times explain part of the attraction of the bestselling *Left Behind* novels. Tens of millions of copies have sold, along with related merchandise such as spin-off books, T-shirts, and video games. The first novel in the series, *Left Behind: A Novel of the Earth's Last Days* (1995), begins with passengers aboard an airplane disappearing from their seats. *Kingdom Come,* the sixteenth and final novel in the series, ends with the appearance of Christ at the close of the battle of Armageddon.

It seems that everyone wonders about the Last Things. But those who carefully study the Bible have a unique glimpse into how things will end. That's because the author of the Bible is the Creator of our universe. He set the stars in motion. He created human life. And he knows how things will conclude.

Unveiling the Mystery

Our word *apocalypse* comes from the New Testament Greek word *apokalupsis,* which means "to reveal" or "to unveil." Both the Old and New Testaments of the Bible contain passages that give insights into the consummation of this age. Some people like to read these passages in isolation from one another. But a better way is to read them together, allowing these various passages to give a more complete picture of how our world will end.

These passages agree on one thing: our age will end with a time of great trial and tribulation. Movies and novels have spun these passages into a series of horrifying visions of the end. And while history may not conclude with all the technicolored explosions and gore we've come to expect on the movie screen, rough times are ahead for the human race.

Some people dwell on these passages to scare and frighten people. In this chapter, we study these passages to instead be informed and prepared for the future. In doing so, we can move from a position of irrational fear to one of rational concern.

In some ways, the Bible paints a picture more harrowing and hellish than anything film could capture. In part, that's because many of the biblical passages about the Last Things are written in metaphorical language.

We use metaphors all the time. When you describe a day at work as a "grind," or a football game as a "barn burner," you're applying an emotionally evocative word or phrase to something else for comparative purposes, but not to be taken literally. Likewise, biblical writers employed metaphors to paint pictures of the end.

The word pictures they created can rival the depictions of some of the most shocking tragedies of human history. Perhaps you've studied the Black Death, or Black Plague, which, during the fourteenth century, killed one-third of Europe's population and millions more in Asia. The Crusades pitted Christians against Muslims until the streets of Jerusalem ran red with blood. World War II saw the destruction of much of

Europe as well as the Holocaust of millions of Jews and other innocent victims. The terrorist attacks of 9/11 and the shootings of innocent young people at Columbine High School and Virginia Tech are shocking tragedies of more recent days.

The apocalypse revealed in the Bible is, in some ways, more horrifying than any of these tragedies. But another, more hopeful dimension of the story comes through many of these passages as well. Within the accounts of suffering and chaos are portraits of faith, prayer, love, and joy. The Bible that reveals the horrors of the Last Things is the same Bible that reveals something much more powerful and amazing: the hope God gives us to persevere, no matter how bad things get.

Revelations of the End

The first passage we examine comes from the prophet Daniel.

> At that time shall arise Michael, the great prince who has charge of your people. And there shall be a time of trouble, such as never has been since there was a nation till that time. But at that time your people shall be delivered, everyone whose name shall be found written in the book. And many of those who sleep in the dust of the earth shall awake, some to everlasting life, and some to shame and everlasting contempt. And those who are wise shall shine like the brightness of the sky above; and those who turn many to righteousness, like the stars forever and ever. But you, Daniel, shut up the words and seal the book, until the time of the end. Many shall run to and fro, and

knowledge shall increase. Then I, Daniel, looked, and behold, two others stood, one on this bank of the stream and one on that bank of the stream. And someone said to the man clothed in linen, who was above the waters of the stream, "How long shall it be till the end of these wonders?" And I heard the man clothed in linen, who was above the waters of the stream; he raised his right hand and his left hand toward heaven and swore by him who lives forever that it would be for a time, times, and half a time, and that when the shattering of the power of the holy people comes to an end all these things would be finished. I heard, but I did not understand. Then I said, "O my lord, what shall be the outcome of these things?" He said, "Go your way, Daniel, for the words are shut up and sealed until the time of the end. Many shall purify themselves and make themselves white and be refined, but the wicked shall act wickedly. And none of the wicked shall understand, but those who are wise shall understand. And from the time that the regular burnt offering is taken away and the abomination that makes desolate is set up, there shall be 1,290 days. Blessed is he who waits and arrives at the 1,335 days. But go your way till the end. And you shall rest and shall stand in your allotted place at the end of the days." (Daniel 12:1–13 ESV)

Another key passage comes from Mark's gospel. Jesus' Olivet Discourse took place on the Mount of Olives, an important location previously visited by King David, the prophet Ezekiel, and others. It was probably on the Mount of Olives near Bethany that Jesus raised Lazarus from the dead. Here is part of Jesus' Olivet Discourse:

> For in those days there will be such tribulation as has not been from the beginning of the creation that God created until now, and never will be. And if the Lord had not cut short the days, no human being would be saved. But for the sake of the elect, whom he chose, he shortened the days. But in those days, after that tribulation, the sun will be darkened, and the moon will not give its light, and the stars will be falling from heaven, and the powers in the heavens will be shaken. And then they will see the Son of man coming in clouds with great power and glory. And then he will send out the angels and gather his elect from the four winds, from the ends of the earth to the ends of heaven. (Mark 13:19–20, 24–27 ESV)

We could look at many similar passages. For example, in Deuteronomy 4, Moses prophesies a coming time of great tribulation. The word *tribulation* comes from the Latin word *tribulum*, which describes a piece of agricultural equipment used in the ancient Roman world to separate wheat from chaff through a violent vibrating process called *tribulatio*. The meaning is that Earth itself will one day shake and experience great tribulation.

Other key passages can be found in 1 and 2 Timothy, 1 and 2 Thessalonians, 2 Peter 3, and, of course, John's

Revelation, particularly chapters 6–18. As we study these passages, a picture of the end will begin to emerge.

Although much about this subject can cause disagreements and even arguments, most scholars agree that the Last Days will feature the seven "signs of the times" described below.

Sign 1: A Time of Peace

You may find this sign of peace surprising, since we just read of a coming time of trouble and shaking. But as the book of Revelation makes clear, when the Antichrist (see chapter six of this book) rises to power, he will come with an offer of peace. Various nations of the world will sign a peace treaty with Israel, and the world will applaud the outbreak of peace in this heretofore-troubled land.

But as is true with many treaties, this one will not be worth the paper on which it is signed. The Antichrist will break his covenant, and the peace will fail. The Bible tells us that *after* people believe peace and security are finally possible, sudden destruction shall come on them, much as travail comes upon a woman in childbirth. After these promises of peace, the tribulation will explode in force.

Sign 2: Cosmic Disturbances

The second characteristic of the tribulation is cosmic disturbances that affect events on Earth. In Revelation 6:13, we read, "the stars of the sky fell to the earth as the fig tree sheds its winter fruit when shaken by a gale" (ESV). Meanwhile, the sun will not give its light.

An example could be an asteroid heading toward Earth, as portrayed in the movie *Armageddon*. Such events have happened before. Geologists say an asteroid collided with this planet thousands of years ago, between the Cretaceous and Tertiary periods of Earth's history, resulting in the demise of dinosaurs and the eradication of half the life on Earth. This may or may not be the sort of thing that characterizes the tribulation period, but we know there will be earthly destruction with a cosmic causation. Something *out there* will have a major impact on what happens *here*.

Sign 3: Earthly Disturbances

The third characteristic of the great tribulation will be earthly disturbances that are unrelated to cosmic disturbances. These include earthquakes, volcanoes, tsunamis, and other overwhelming forces in nature.

Countless earthquakes in recent years have shaken our planet. A 1976 earthquake in China killed nearly 250,000 people. An undersea earthquake caused the 2004 tsunami that killed 230,000 people in fourteen countries. Even more recently, a January 2010 earthquake devastated the nation of Haiti. Scriptures tell us the disturbances that rage around the world during the great tribulation will be much worse than any of the highly destructive earthquakes we've seen to date.

In Revelation, the final trumpet judgment is an earthquake—the greatest earthquake in the history of the world. Islands will descend into the sea, and mountains will fall into the ocean. These geological disasters will, of course, greatly affect the earth's population.

Today, some scientists say that global warming is the cause of the increased severity and frequency of tropical storms. I'm not qualified to assess the scientific debate surrounding global warming, but I deeply believe that God's call for us to be stewards of his creation means that we should work toward solving environmental degradation. (For example, on our recent mission trip to Belize, we discussed the effects on the environment of deforestation.)

But even the most horrific scenarios in Al Gore's movie, *An Inconvenient Truth,* will pale in comparison to the natural disasters that will occur during the tribulation. Revelation 16:8–9 says the world will experience an unprecedented heating of the sun and scorching of the earth: "The fourth angel poured out his bowl on the sun, and it was allowed to scorch people with fire. They were scorched by the fierce heat, and they cursed the name of God who had power over these plagues. They did not repent and give him glory" (ESV). These earthly disturbances will render the earth uninhabitable for millions of its residents.

Sign 4: Famine

Bread for the World is a Christian movement that seeks justice for the world's hungry people by lobbying U.S. decision makers. The group's website (www.bread.org/learn/hunger-basics/hunger-facts-international.html) contains startling facts about hunger in our world today: almost 1 trillion people around the world are hungry, and a child dies of hunger-related causes every five seconds.

Famine is a horrible thing to endure. None of us in the overfed-West can imagine what it's like. But throughout human history, many civilizations have disappeared because of famine. These things will only be worse at the end of the age. Even people who have enjoyed plenty of food will suffer the pangs of hunger.

Many passages in the Bible, including Revelation 6:5–8 and Matthew 24:7, tell us that famine will be a sign of the tribulation, that many people will pay a day's wage for a loaf of bread.

> When the Lamb opened the third seal, I heard the third living creature say, "Come!" I looked, and there before me was a black horse! Its rider was holding a pair of scales in his hand. Then I heard what sounded like a voice among the four living creatures, saying, "Two pounds of wheat for a day's wages, and six pounds of barley for a day's wages, and do not damage the oil and the wine!" When the Lamb opened the fourth seal, I heard the voice of the fourth living creature say, "Come!" I looked, and there before me was a pale horse! Its rider was named Death, and Hades was following close behind him. They were given power over a fourth of the earth to kill by sword, famine and plague, and by the wild beasts of the earth. (Revelation 6:5–8 TNIV)

Archaeologists and historians have researched a group of people called the Acadians. This advanced civilization flourished some four thousand years ago in an area near modern-day Iraq—until they suddenly vanished from the face of the earth. The consensus is that the Acadians disappeared because of famine and global climate changes that affected their region. People left their farms to move to cities, where officials raised the city walls ever higher to protect food supplies from desperate invaders.

As we reach the end of the age, such scenarios will be repeated, but on a global scale.

Sign 5: Pestilence

The movie *Outbreak* shows what could happen if a fatal virus became airborne and infected the countryside. Beginning in the fictional town of Cedar Creek, California, where the virus first appears, the film moves to the halls of government in Washington, D.C., where leaders debate the ethics of bombing Cedar Creek in an effort to contain the contagion (and, incidentally, cover a conspiracy).

"As I understand it, you want to firebomb the town of Cedar Creek, population 2,600, with something called a fuel air bomb, the most powerful non-nuclear weapon in our arsenal," says one irate official at a tense government meeting. "The way it works, it implodes, sucks in all available oxygen to the core, vaporizes everything within a mile of Ground Zero, men, women, children and one airborne virus. Destruction complete. Case closed. Crisis over."

The official can't believe others want to pursue such a deadly proposal. But without quick action, the virus would spread across the country within forty-eight hours.

Pestilence is the fifth sign of the tribulation. On a much smaller scale, we've seen viral outbreaks travel from Asia to Western countries in a matter of weeks. In these instances, we've done what we could to protect ourselves, whether staying away from crowds, receiving a vaccine, or wearing a protective mask.

But according to the Bible, it will be more difficult for the human race to protect itself from the pestilence that will rack the earth in the final tribulation. This will be an era of widespread disease and death, so the ways we prepare ourselves will be radically different from anything we've done in the past.

Sign 6: War

World War II was supposedly the war to end all wars. The decades since have demonstrated this to be an overly optimistic prediction. The current war on terrorism shows how war is changing: instead of one country's army fighting another country's army, independent militias and radical groups wreak havoc on innocent civilians.

And, the reasons people battle each other are ever new and changing. In some regions, the scarcity of water makes new wars possible. Some speculate that battles will erupt even over who controls access to the planets and moons in our solar system. And what will happen if global warming leads to melting of the polar ice caps? Among other things, there will be conflicts over ownership of and access to new sea routes opened after the ice disappears.

Five thousand years of human history records very few years of peace. Perhaps we have grown used to hearing about nations at war. Still, war is given as a sign of the end times. We can expect wars to continue, and as we grow closer to the end of the age, we will see even greater tensions among peoples and nations. There will be many small skirmishes and major wars, all of them leading to the largest battle ever on our planet—the battle of Armageddon

Sign 7: Persecution

The final sign of the great tribulation is persecution and martyrdom of those faithful to Christ and of those who come to faith in him during the tribulation. Their faith will be challenged as forces of the Antichrist persecute God's faithful ones.

Christians have faced persecution since the earliest days of the church, but signs indicate that things may be getting worse. In 2002, a book entitled *The New Persecuted* argued that, of the 70 million Christians martyred throughout history, an estimated 45 million of those died for their faith during the twentieth century.

Is this a sign of the end? Or does the increase, worldwide, in Christians facing persecution merely reflect the rise in global population? No one can answer these questions with certainty. But we can say that the end times will bring unprecedented trials and tribulations.

The picture of the great tribulation to come is not pleasant. Neither is it fun to contemplate death and destruction on such a massive scale. But the Bible is true and trustworthy. Severe tribulation is coming. We will see the wrath, indignation, and judgment of a Holy God, along with the satanic wrath of the Devil and the Antichrist. And we will see the wrath of humanity, which is rarely righteous.

The next few chapters look more closely at specific things believers will need to do before and during these times. But first, I want to balance the tales of horror and suffering we've explored so far with a message of hope and comfort, which also resonates in these biblical passages.

From Signs of the Times to Signs of Hope

It's important to understand what the Bible says about the Last Things. It's equally important to realize that these tales of trouble and woe are not the whole story. The same Bible that promises horrors also promises hope to those who remain true to our God. "In the world you will have tribulation," Jesus told us, before adding, "But be of good cheer, I have overcome the world" (John 16:33 NKJV). What does this hope look like?

We all experience pressure, stress, affliction, and trouble, don't we? You may be experiencing economic stress right now. You may be afflicted physically. Perhaps you're struggling with a disease, and maybe it's life threatening. You may be in pain relationally or emotionally, because life is not easy.

It seems that no matter who we are, while we have many times of joy, we also have times of sadness. The good news? God has overcome the world.

This generation may be the final one. Or perhaps it won't be. You may live to see the great tribulation. Or perhaps you won't. All these things are *outside* our control. So, let's focus on what *is within* our control: how we live our lives.

In whatever days or years you and I have remaining, we are called to live in faithfulness to God. And, we must continually grow in our faith, no matter what happens in our lives.

There's a prayer that can guide us as we face the challenges of the present and the horrors of the future. The prayer is so familiar we may have lost sight of its power and insight. Will you pray the Lord's Prayer with me right now?

> Our Father in heaven, hallowed be Thy name. Thy kingdom come. Thy will be done on earth as it is in heaven. Give us this day our daily bread. Forgive us our sins as we forgive those who sin against us. Lead us not into testing or temptation but deliver us from evil for Thine is the kingdom and the power and the glory forever. Amen. (Matthew 6:9–13, author's paraphrase)

If you feel overcome by the burdens and woes of life, write this prayer on a card and tape it to your mirror, your refrigerator, or your computer. When you feel your concerns rising and threatening to get out of hand, repeat this prayer, which has brought comfort to so many over the centuries.

Perhaps you're concerned about the things we've discussed in this chapter. That's understandable. But if your concerns turn into fears, I suggest you repeat the following prayer until its comforting truth resonates throughout your soul. Will you join me?

> Lord Jesus, we don't like to think about the great tribulation. But you've shown us in your Word that it is coming on this earth. We would love you to take us out of the world before then, but we want to be faithful, no matter what you call us to do. Lord, help us to serve you faithfully as long as we draw breath, come what may. Keep us faithful to you until we see you face to face. Amen.

Bad times are coming. But a good God loves us all. He promises not to leave us alone, no matter whether the tribulations we face are ordinary and mundane or cataclysmic and apocalyptic. Jesus has overcome the world, and that truth is our source of joy and faith.

— 5 —

APOSTASY:

FALSE IDEAS AND FAULTY LIVES

Has anyone ever turned his or her back on you? Perhaps a promise was made, a handshake given, or a contract signed. But when push came to shove, the commitment in which you had placed so much trust evaporated into thin air.

A citizen who turns her back on her country is called a traitor. A soldier who turns his back on his comrades-in-arms is called a deserter. And followers of Jesus who turn their back on the Lord are called apostates.

Apostasy is nothing new. In the fourth century, the Roman emperor Julian turned a whole empire away from faith in Christ. His uncle Constantine had done many things to promote Christianity. But after Julian ascended to the throne in 361, he turned his back on his upbringing in the faith. He reestablished throughout the Roman Empire the worship of pagan gods, and he reinstituted the persecution of those who followed Jesus. That's why history now refers to this ruler as Julian the Apostate.

You and I face the same challenge as Julian the Apostate: to remain faithful to Jesus, or to turn our back on him. As we grow closer to the end of the age, apostasy will take a greater toll on believers worldwide.

Two Ways to Turn Away

The Bible uses a variety of words to describe the concept of apostasy. For example, the Hebrew word *mesuba* can refer to rebellion against one's country or one's God. In Hebrews 6:4, we find the word *peripipto* in the book's discussion of those "who have tasted the heavenly gift" before committing apostasy against Jesus Christ. The Greek word *apostasia* is actually the source of our English word "apostasy." In Acts 21:21, apostasia refers to the Hebrew people who turned against Moses. In 2 Thessalonians 2, it refers to those who turn against Christ. In this passage, Paul says: "Concerning the coming of our Lord Jesus Christ and our assembling to meet him, . . . Let no one deceive you in any way; for that day will not come, unless the rebellion comes first." Here the Greek word apostasia is translated "rebellion."

There are numerous ways to turn our backs on another person. As the time of the Last Things draws near, two forms of apostasy will become increasingly common. One form involves the things *we think and believe*—doctrinal apostasy. The other involves the things *we do*—moral apostasy.

Let's examine these forms of apostasy, so that we don't turn our backs on God, today or in the future.

Doctrinal Apostasy

In 2 Timothy 4:3–4, Paul says, "For the time will come when people will not put up with sound doctrine. Instead, to suit their own desires, they will gather around them a great number of teachers to say what their itching ears want to hear. They will turn their ears away from the truth and turn aside to myths" (TNIV). He also writes that, eventually, these "will fall away from the faith, paying attention to deceitful spirits and doctrines of demons" (1 Timothy 4:1 NASB).

Christians obviously disagree on some points. But there is widespread agreement on the fundamentals of the faith, the sound biblical doctrines that have been handed down to us, generation after generation, since the time of Christ. These fundamentals are summarized in the Apostles' Creed, a statement that originated with the baptismal rituals of the earliest Christians and was written down and formally adopted by the entire church. Before individuals could be baptized, they had to affirm their belief in these foundational doctrines of the faith.

> I believe in God, the Father Almighty, the Creator of heaven and earth, and in Jesus Christ, His only Son, our Lord: Who was conceived of the Holy Spirit, born of the Virgin Mary, suffered under Pontius Pilate, was crucified, died, and was buried. He descended into hell. The third day He arose again from the dead. He ascended into heaven and sits at the right hand of God the Father Almighty, whence He shall come to judge the living and the dead. I believe in the Holy Spirit, the holy Catholic Church, the communion of saints, the

forgiveness of sins, the resurrection of the body, and life everlasting. Amen.

Creeds have been important in stating and protecting sound doctrine and in warding off apostasy in the church and in institutions.

Cherry Hills Christian, the school program operated by our church, carefully and intentionally follows a statement of faith (http://www.cherryhillschristian.org/about/faith.php) that reaffirms many of the elements of the classic Christian creeds. We're well aware that over the years other schools have lost their founding values.

Take Harvard University for example. Over the centuries, the university has drifted from its original purpose and its founding commitment to the truth. *Veritas,* the Latin word for "truth," first appeared in a design for the school insignia in 1643. Historian Samuel Eliot Morison wrote in *Three Centuries of Harvard* that the motto "undoubtedly meant (as it did to Dante) the divine truth." A Harvard insignia of 1650 bears the motto *In Christi Gloriam* (For the Glory of Christ), and an insignia created in 1692 reads *Christo et Ecclesiæ* (Truth for Christ and the Church). But in recent centuries, Harvard University has drifted from its commitment to divine truth as well as from its mission to train students for Christian service. The institution is now secular.

A similar thing has happened at Princeton University. The school's flag still contains the words *Vet Nov Testamentum,* which means "Old and New Testament." And the slogan on the flag reads, "Under the providence of God we shall prevail." But like Harvard, Princeton has drifted from its founding commitment and today is a secular institution.

Closer to home, for decades, I've watched with frustration the denomination in which I was originally ordained drift into apostasy. That denomination has questioned the deity of Jesus, ordained practicing homosexuals, and redefined the Trinity. This saddens me, and the denomination's movement away from sound doctrine is a major reason Cherry Hills Community Church is affiliated with the Evangelical Presbyterian Church (EPC).

The EPC denomination has remained faithful to sound doctrine, both the Apostles' Creed and the Westminster Confession of Faith (written in 1646). The Westminster Confession, an important creed for Protestants, covers a number of key topics, including Scripture, the Holy Trinity, the fall of humanity and salvation, Christian liberty, worship, marriage, other sacraments of the church, and the last judgment.

Why do I spend time talking about the mottos of Harvard and Princeton and about centuries-old creedal statements? Because Christianity is not something we make up on our own. It is a tradition that affirms specific biblical beliefs. If we fail to affirm those beliefs in our lives and in our churches, we are on our way to apostasy.

The historical Christian creeds are like mission statements in a business. In some businesses, daily operations have nothing to do with principles written years ago. But if we are to be true and faithful to the God we say we serve and love, we need to constantly measure our beliefs and our actions against the standards passed to us by earlier generations of Christian leaders.

Many Paths to Doctrinal Error

Some of our culture's most popular views about religion can lead people away from the truth at the heart of Christian doctrine. One of these views is "pluralism." You may be unfamiliar with the term, but you have undoubtedly heard its philosophy expressed like this: "There are many paths to God."

Pluralists believe that there are many paths to God and that all religions of the world are pretty much the same as well as equally true. Pluralism is an affront to God who, in the Ten Commandments, said: "You shall have no other gods besides me."

A pluralist can claim to believe in God and Christian teaching while also claiming to believe in other things that directly contradict Christian doctrine. That's why pluralists are often very uncomfortable with evangelism and missions. After all, why should we worry ourselves about fulfilling Christ's Great Commission if all paths leading to God are equally valid and true? This is a modern form of apostasy.

"Syncretism" is another contemporary heresy. Syncretists take bits of various religions and try to combine them into a new spiritual package that seems right for them. Some call it a "cafeteria religion," one in which you go down the line and take a little bit of this religion and a little bit of that one. Syncretists may like some aspects of Jesus' life and teachings, but when they combine Jesus with various unbiblical, non-Christian concepts, they run into trouble.

For example, some people embrace a loving Jesus, but reject the idea of Jesus as judge, though it is an important part of the New Testament picture. Some syncretists move away from the biblical emphasis on judgment to favor the Eastern-religion concept of karma. In combining religious beliefs, they have walked away from biblical theology.

I think of syncretism as the theological equivalent to the platypus. Have you ever taken a good look at a platypus? It has a flat tail like a beaver, but the webbed feet and bill of a duck. It has venomous poison like a snake, but it's not a snake. It can swim like a fish, but it's not a fish. It lays eggs like a bird, but it's not a bird. Zoologists aren't sure how to categorize this animal. That's the problem theologians have with syncretism. It's such a mix of various beliefs and traditions that it fails to show decisive features of biblical truth. It doesn't fit any of them very well.

What do you believe? What do your children believe?

Christian Smith and his team of researchers spent years examining the beliefs of young people who attended youth groups in Christian churches. When these kids described their core beliefs, Smith was shocked. In his 2005 book, *Soul Searching: The Religious and Spiritual Lives of American Teenagers* (Oxford University Press), Smith says that the theology of many "Christian" teens could be described as "moralistic therapeutic deism." The dominant beliefs are these: God wants us to be good and feel good. God is there for us when we need his help, but he stays out of our lives if that's what we want. And if we're morally good, we'll go to heaven when we die.

Moralistic therapeutic deism is another contemporary form of syncretism. It's also a contemporary form of apostasy, since it departs from the biblical doctrines that have formed the core of Christian teaching for twenty centuries.

I don't know what new forms of apostasy will appear as we get closer to the end of the age, but it seems we may have a head start on the doctrinal apostasy the Bible says will be a feature of the Last Things. If some believers are already sacrificing core Christian beliefs, things will only get worse as times grow more troubling for the church of Jesus Christ.

Moral Apostasy

We may say, "How can people believe crazy stuff like that?" We may even pat ourselves on the back because we believe all the right things. But how do we *live,* moment-by-moment, day-by-day? If we don't practice the things we say we believe, then we could fall victim to moral apostasy, which is the second way to turn away from the bedrock truths of Christianity.

Some people are confused in their *thinking*: they don't know what they believe, which defines doctrinal apostasy, as discussed above. Other people believe the right things, but they're confused in their *living*: they say the right things, but they don't practice their beliefs, which is moral apostasy. It, too, will grow more prevalent as we approach the Last Things.

A number of Bible passages say the end of the age will witness an increase of "lawlessness." This refers not to people who break laws of the state, but to people who disobey the moral laws of God. The apostle John explains in 1 John 3:4: "Everyone who commits sin is guilty of lawlessness; sin is lawlessness." At the end of the age, sin will increase, although, as Paul wrote in 2 Thessalonians 2:7, "the mystery of lawlessness is already at work."

Jesus is concerned with moral apostasy, particularly within churches. Sometimes we look back longingly to the early days of the church and say, "Wouldn't it be great to live back then, when the faith was so pure and powerful?" But if we read Revelation 2 and 3, we'll hear Jesus criticizing these early congregations. He warned the church in Pergamum about its moral apostasy. He warned them about the Balaamites and the Nicolaitans—moral libertines who lived the motto, "If it feels good, do it." These people had infiltrated the churches, and Jesus warned his followers that judgment would fall on them if they did not flee this moral apostasy.

Jesus also spoke to the church in Thyatira, warning them against the Jezebelites, affiliated with the cult of Jezebel. He said the church was tolerating false teachers who promoted sexual immorality. This is moral apostasy, and Jesus hates it.

But before we point our fingers at these early believers, let's look around us. Here in North America there is great moral apostasy—sexual immorality, drunkenness, gluttony, lack of commitment to spouse or children, dishonesty at work, and a continual search for new and pleasing sensations.

One of the words Jesus used when he addressed his message to Thyatira was *porneia,* which referred to sex before marriage, adultery (the violation of marriage vows), and homosexuality. From pornea, we get our word *pornography,* a sin that is rampant in our so-called Christian nation.

In fact, some say that 90 percent of the world's output of pornography is produced right here in the United States. And one-third of our Internet usage is porn-related. We live in times of moral apostasy. Surely, God's judgment cannot be far away.

Law or Love?

If you grew up in a legalistic or fundamentalist church setting, then perhaps you focus on breaking God's laws as we discuss moral apostasy. God's laws are an important part of the picture, but they are not the whole picture.

God wants us to obey his moral commands, but ultimately, moral apostasy is the abandonment of love. Anyone who falls into moral apostasy does not love God as the Bible directs us. Instead, he or she loves something or someone more than God.

Jesus sent a message to the church at Ephesus, saying, "But I have this against you, that you have abandoned the love you had at first" (Revelation 2:4 ESV). In other words, he told them that, by forsaking their first love, they had committed moral apostasy. There are many other places in the Bible where we see the connection between love and moral living. In Mark 12, Jesus quoted Deuteronomy 6 and Leviticus 19 when he answered a question about the greatest commandment. "You shall love the Lord your God with all your heart," he said, and "You shall love your neighbor as yourself." Jesus showed us that all the commandments of God can be summed up in one word—love.

Matthew 25 teaches that love will determine our eternal destiny.

> When the Son of man comes in his glory, and all the angels with him, then he will sit on his glorious throne. Before him will be gathered all the nations, and he will separate them one from another as a shepherd separates the sheep from the goats, and he will place the sheep at his right

hand, but the goats at the left.

Then the King will say to those at his right hand, "Come, O blessed of my Father, inherit the kingdom prepared for you from the foundation of the world; for I was hungry and you gave me food, I was thirsty and you gave me drink, I was a stranger and you welcomed me, I was naked and you clothed me, I was sick and you visited me, I was in prison and you came to me."

Then the righteous will answer him, "Lord, when did we see thee hungry and feed thee, or thirsty and give thee drink? And when did we see thee a stranger and welcome thee, or naked and clothe thee? And when did we see thee sick or in prison and visit thee?"

And the King will answer them, "Truly, I say to you, as you did it to one of the least of these my brethren, you did it to me."

Then he will say to those at his left hand, "Depart from me, you cursed, into the eternal fire prepared for the devil and his angels; for I was hungry and you gave me no food, I was thirsty and you gave me no drink, I was a stranger and you did not welcome me, naked and you did not clothe me, sick and in prison and you did not visit me."

Then they also will answer, "Lord, when did we see thee hungry or thirsty or a stranger or naked or sick or in prison, and did not minister to thee?"

> Then he will answer them, "Truly, I say to
> you, as you did it not to one of the least of these,
> you did it not to me."
>
> And they will go away into eternal punish-
> ment, but the righteous into eternal life. (Matthew
> 25:31–46)

Here, Jesus emphasizes love, not law. By not caring for those who were thirsty, naked, or in prison, people who thought they were following Christ failed to love others. In so doing, they failed to love Jesus our Lord and so were guilty of moral apostasy.

For those raised on a steady diet of lectures on all the bad stuff we shouldn't do, don't forget that Jesus is just as concerned with how we love. Why? Because Jesus knows that loving God will keep us from doing bad things. Love protects us from moral apostasy.

If you're dabbling in apostasy or pornea in any of their varied forms, the message for you is the same as the message Jesus gave those early churches. The time to repent is now. Maybe you can recite the Apostle's Creed backward and forward. But do you live it in your life and your love? If not, moral apostasy is lurking in the shadows, seeking an opening in your soul.

A Fountain of Love and Blessing

Robert Robinson lived in the eighteenth century, and his story illustrates the redeeming power of God's love. If Robinson were alive today, we would call him a party animal. When he was seventeen years old, he and his friends visited the city of London. After a few days of drinking, the group visited a fortuneteller. Afterward, Robinson felt troubled by his drunkenness and sorcery.

He attended a meeting featuring the famous revivalist George Whitefield, who shared the gospel of Jesus Christ, called people to repentance, and gave an invitation for salvation. Robinson accepted the invitation and asked Jesus into his heart. But he felt troubled about this, too. So later, when he was sober, he recommitted his life to Christ.

Following his recommitment, Robinson wrote one of the great hymns of the faith, "Come Thou Fount of Every Blessing." The hymn thanks God for streams of mercy and love that never ceases. Robinson himself was soon able to test the truth of these words.

After he wrote this powerful hymn, Robinson renounced his faith in Christ and returned to a wild lifestyle. One day in Paris, he saw a woman he wanted to take to bed. When he approached her and asked her out, she responded by inviting him to an event she would be attending that night. Robinson thought he was well on his way to another affair. Instead, he found himself at a prayer meeting—where people were singing his hymn, "Come Thou Fount of Every Blessing."

Hearing the words he had once held so dear tore him apart and he began to weep. When the woman asked what was wrong, he told her, "I wrote that song years ago, but I've left the path." She told him, "The streams of mercy are still flowing, and the fount of God's redeeming love is still there." Robinson recommitted his life to Jesus Christ that night.

What about you? Are you guilty of doctrinal apostasy? Have you left the truth of God for the doctrines of demons?

Or maybe you can recite all the right creeds and Bible verses, but your life is a moral black hole. Have you wandered away from the path of godly living for the easy street of moral apostasy?

Either way, you don't need to wait for the end of the age to straighten out your life. Lawlessness is already at work in the world, but you don't have to be seduced by that power.

Instead, let yourself fall madly in love with God and experience the depth of his fountain of many blessings.

— 6 —

OUR ENEMY, THE ANTICHRIST

A Google search of the word *antichrist* generates about 8 million matches. I think the sheer number of search results reveals much about the freewheeling diversity of our contemporary religious and cultural scenes. Some of these search results included

- antichrist websites sponsored by obscure religious groups
- websites sponsored by nonreligious, atheist groups
- websites compiled by those who say they've received messages from aliens in outer space
- references to mass murderers, such as Charles Manson
- information about shock-rock artist Marilyn Manson, who recorded an album called *Antichrist Superstar*
- websites claiming that the antichrist was embodied

in diverse historical figures, such as Friedrich
Nietzsche, George W. Bush, and a variety of popes
• a website about an antichrist computer-virus hoax

A few years ago, the blogosphere and the news media covered a Guatemalan religious figure named Jose Luis de Jesus Miranda. Miranda sometimes referred to himself as the Antichrist and sported a 666 tattoo. He even formed a small movement of followers devoted to the concept of him as God.

Clearly, the biblical term "antichrist" has been woven throughout our culture and our collective subconscious to such a degree that it's difficult for us to quiet our imaginations and focus our minds on what the Bible actually says about this controversial but important topic. We'll try to do just that in this chapter.

Mysteries, Names, and Numbers

As with other aspects of the Last Things, multiple passages in the Bible provide insights into the Antichrist—the name given to the ultimate man of sin who will arise in the last days. Focusing on 2 Thessalonians 2, Revelation 13, Daniel 7, and other passages, we'll piece together a biblically based picture, which will be different from many of the concepts prevalent in our culture. Unfortunately, after examining these passages, we'll still face a number of mysteries that are unanswered in the Bible.

We know from the epistles of John that the Greek word *antichristos* means either "against Christ" or "in place of Christ." And in some sense, both of these meanings will be true. The Antichrist will indeed be against Christ, and he will seek to take the place of Christ by becoming a new king of kings.

The apostle Paul, in 2 Thessalonians 2:3, called the Antichrist the "man of lawlessness," which means "without law" or "without moral law." He is also known as the man of sin and the son of perdition. In Revelation 13, the Antichrist is also called "the beast"; indeed, the Greek term the apostle John used here typically refers to a wild animal. In Daniel 7, the Antichrist is called "the little horn." In ancient times, a horn was symbolic of kingly power.

We also know that the Antichrist is bound for "ruin" or "destruction," though this will happen only after unimagined ruin and destruction have been loosed on the earth.

What we don't know with precision is his name. Revelation 13 says, "The number of the beast is 666," but scholars, for nearly twenty centuries, have disagreed over what this means.

In the first century, many Christians believed Nero, emperor of the Roman Empire, was the Antichrist. Nero, the fifth and last emperor of the Julio-Claudian dynasty, was a man with a twisted soul. He murdered his own parents. He murdered his brother. He murdered his pregnant wife. For his own amusement, Nero tortured Christians throughout the Roman world, rolling some in tar and setting them on fire at night, as human torches. He wrapped Christians in animal flesh and fed them to packs of wild dogs.

Many Christians at the time believed Nero's behavior matched what they would expect of an antichrist. Even after the death of Nero, many believed in a strange doctrine called

"Nero Redivivas," which stated that Nero would somehow come back to life.

When the Greek name "Neron Caesar" was transliterated into Hebrew, the letters added up to 666. Since then, people have tried to convert various human names into some scheme that could equal 666. It's relatively easy to do. If you want to make someone's name add up to 666, try doing the math on letters in Greek. If that doesn't work, try Hebrew. If that doesn't work, you could try Swedish. The truth is that it's easy to make almost any name equate numerically to 666.

During the Protestant Reformation of the sixteenth century, reformers such as Martin Luther and John Calvin believed that the Antichrist would be a corrupt pope. By that time, there had certainly been some corrupt popes. And, the words "Italian church" in Greek could add up to 666. But turnabout is fair play. Some in the Catholic leadership said they had found a way to make "Martin Luther" add up to 666!

Anti-Catholicism did not disappear after the Reformation. When John F. Kennedy ran for president in 1960, some Protestant leaders claimed that the Catholic Kennedy would be the means through which the pope would finally exert control over the world. It didn't help that Kennedy received 666 votes at the Democratic Convention. (Later, Democrats fought back by raising questions about Republican President Ronald Wilson Reagan, whose three names had six letters each. In addition, the Reagan's Bellaire home in California was on 666 St. Cloud Drive. Nancy Reagan changed the address to 668 to avoid further demonization.) Playing tricks with numbers doesn't really help us unravel mysteries about the Antichrist. It only muddies the water.

Some imaginative people have tried to twist Scripture and math to show that other historical figures were the Antichrist, including Nazi leader Adolph Hitler, Iraqi dictator Saddam Hussein, Russian leader Mikhail S. Gorbachev, and even Microsoft founder Bill Gates.

Another mystery surrounds the personhood of the Antichrist. In addition to being referred to by the number 666, which is unusual enough, we can't be sure if this figure is a single person or some other kind of entity. Sometimes the Antichrist is called "he" and sometimes "it" or "they." The Antichrist, however, is never "she," so women are off the hook.

The personhood issue may cause confusion for some, but some scholars argue that the Antichrist can actually be both "he" and "it." The pronoun *he* could imply references to the "man of lawlessness." The pronoun *it* could imply references to the spirit of the antichrist that the Bible says is already at work in the world.

So, in a sense, the antichrist is a diabolical or demonic spirit that has been working in the world, and in all cultures, throughout human history. Of course, this evil work will culminate in the rise of the final Antichrist at the end of history. Meanwhile, people will continue to speculate.

But not everything about the Antichrist is a mystery. In fact, we can know two truths with certainty about this person.

The Pursuit of Power

The Bible makes it very clear: the Antichrist is motivated by power. He longs to acquire and exercise power over people, and even over the entire world.

> Now concerning the coming of our Lord Jesus Christ and our being gathered together to him, we ask you, brothers, not to be quickly shaken in mind or alarmed, either by a spirit or a spoken word, or a letter seeming to be from us, to the effect that the day of the Lord has come. Let no one deceive you in any way. For that day will not come, unless the rebellion comes first, and the man of lawlessness is revealed, the son of destruction, who opposes and exalts himself against every so-called god or object of worship, so that he takes his seat in the temple of God, proclaiming himself to be God. Do you not remember that when I was still with you I told you these things? And you know what is restraining him now so that he may be revealed in his time. For the mystery of lawlessness is already at work. Only he who now restrains it will do so until he is out of the way. And then the lawless one will be revealed, whom the Lord Jesus will kill with the breath of his mouth and bring to nothing by the appearance of his coming. The coming of the lawless one is by the activity of Satan with all power and false signs and wonders, and with all wicked deception for those who are perishing,

because they refused to love the truth and so be saved. (2 Thessalonians 2:1–10 ESV)

From this passage, we learn that the Antichrist will exercise the power of Satan in order to do the work of Satan. In Revelation 13:1–4 (ESV), we're told that the dragon (who is the Devil), gives his power to the beast (who is the Antichrist).

> And I saw a beast rising out of the sea, with ten horns and seven heads, with ten diadems on its horns and blasphemous names on its heads. And the beast that I saw was like a leopard; its feet were like a bear's, and its mouth was like a lion's mouth. And to it the dragon gave his power and his throne and great authority. One of its heads seemed to have a mortal wound, but its mortal wound was healed, and the whole earth marveled as they followed the beast. And they worshiped the dragon, for he had given his authority to the beast, and they worshiped the beast, saying, "Who is like the beast, and who can fight against it?"

You may have heard about people who are demon possessed. It's happened many times in history; and, over the years of my ministry, I believe I have encountered a handful of people who were demon possessed. But the Antichrist will be unique. Satan will possess the Antichrist; that is, Satan will work within the personality and body of the Antichrist.

Revelation 13:7 says the Antichrist will seek global power over every tribe and tongue and people and nation. This should not surprise us because Satan longs for global power.

In fact, biblical descriptions of the Antichrist in many ways mirror descriptions of Satan. Isaiah 14 and Ezekiel 28 refer to the fall of Satan at the dawn of time. Satan fell due to his longing and quest for power. He said in his heart, "I will ascend to heaven; above the stars of God I will set my throne on high; I will sit on the mount of assembly in the far north; I will ascend above the heights of the clouds, I will make myself like the Most High" (Isaiah 14:13–14). Power. For both Satan and his co-worker the Antichrist, it's all about power.

The Antichrist's quest for power will lead him to put together a coalition of nations that seek a one-world government. In some ways, descriptions of this one-world government sound similar to descriptions of the Tower of Babel found in Genesis 11. At Babel, humankind, seeking to unite themselves under one language, built an edifice reaching to the heavens. But God is not mocked. He is displeased by our efforts to achieve, in our own energy, a form of unity that can come only through him. So, God rebuked the pride of humanity at Babel. He confused the tongues of the people, giving them various languages, and scattered them around the earth. After Babel, various nations were formed.

The Antichrist will pick up where the people of Babel left off, that is, by trying to create a one-world government. The inspiration for renewing the ancient Tower of Babel will find expression in a global kingdom the Bible calls Babylon. The prophet Daniel even identified the beast with the emergence of this Babylon.

For years, some believers feared that the United Nations (UN) was destined to evolve into this prophesied Babylon. But the UN, which was formed out of the ashes of World War

II, has not tried to act as a one-world government. Rather, it has served as a forum for many nations to discuss and resolve their problems.

Daniel 7–8 and other Scripture passages point to a unified, global government that is far more sinister than the United Nations. In a vision, Daniel saw an empire that would arise with ten horns, representing ten kings or kingdoms. It's impossible to determine what nations or kingdoms these will be. He also saw an eleventh horn, "the little horn," signifying the arrival of the Antichrist.

Daniel's vision then suddenly shifted to the culmination of all things at the end of time. He saw the Son of Man coming on the clouds of heaven. Ultimately, Jesus, who has been given authority and power and dominion over the earth and over the nations, will shatter the power of the eleventh horn, the Antichrist. This triumph will come only after a terrible period of chaos and destruction.

We need to realize that satanic power is not something we can ignore until the end times. This evil power is present in the world today; in fact, the spirit of the antichrist can work in your life and my life if we are seduced by power. If power motivates us, we are playing with fire. The hunger for power comes from the Evil One and the spirit the Bible calls antichrist. This power is the opposite of Christ's teaching: "A dispute also arose among them, which of them was to be regarded as the greatest. And [Jesus] said to them, 'The kings of the Gentiles exercise lordship over them; and those in authority over them are called benefactors. But not so with you; rather let the greatest among you become as the youngest, and the leader as one who serves'" (Luke 22:24–26).

In Philippians, Paul told us:

> Do nothing from selfishness or conceit, but in humility count others better than yourselves. Let each of you look not only to his own interests, but also to the interests of others. Have this mind among yourselves, which is yours in Christ Jesus, who, though he was in the form of God, did not count equality with God a thing to be grasped, but emptied himself, taking the form of a servant, being born in the likeness of men. And being found in human form he humbled himself and became obedient unto death, even death on a cross. (2:3–8)

As followers of Christ, we should walk the earth seeking to serve, not to be served. We should submit ourselves to the power of God, not hoard and abuse power for our own selfish ends. If our minds and hearts aren't clear on this point, we are in danger. If we hunger for power, we may fall under the influence of the spirit of antichrist—either in the present moment or in the final days.

The Hellish Impact of Hate

The second truth we know about the Antichrist is that he is consumed by hatred. In Revelation 12, we read about the wrath of the dragon.

> Now war arose in heaven, Michael and his angels fighting against the dragon. And the dragon and his angels fought back, but he was defeated, and there was no longer any place for them in

heaven. And the great dragon was thrown down, that ancient serpent, who is called the devil and Satan, the deceiver of the whole world—he was thrown down to the earth, and his angels were thrown down with him. And I heard a loud voice in heaven, saying, "Now the salvation and the power and the kingdom of our God and the authority of his Christ have come, for the accuser of our brothers has been thrown down, who accuses them day and night before our God. And they have conquered him by the blood of the Lamb and by the word of their testimony, for they loved not their lives even unto death. Therefore, rejoice, O heavens and you who dwell in them! But woe to you, O earth and sea, for the devil has come down to you in great wrath, because he knows that his time is short!"

And when the dragon saw that he had been thrown down to the earth, he pursued the woman who had given birth to the male child. But the woman was given the two wings of the great eagle so that she might fly from the serpent into the wilderness, to the place where she is to be nourished for a time, and times, and half a time. The serpent poured water like a river out of his mouth after the woman, to sweep her away with a flood. But the earth came to the help of the woman, and the earth opened its mouth and swallowed the river that the dragon had poured from his mouth. Then the dragon became furious

with the woman and went off to make war on the
rest of her offspring, on those who keep the commandments of God and hold to the testimony of
Jesus. And he stood on the sand of the sea. (vv.
7–17 ESV)

The wrath of the Devil is not righteous indignation. It is
pure, unadulterated hate. Satanic wrath is rooted in hate, and
that will be true of the Antichrist as well. He will be fueled by
intense hatred.

Hate is powerful and frightening. We've all felt it at times.
But it's not where most of us live; it is simply a feeling we pass
through on our way to something else, such as forgiveness,
or sorrow, or healing. But when anger settles in and makes
a home in our hearts, all kinds of evil things can take place,
including murder, bitterness, and war.

We've all met people who didn't like us. Well, the Devil
likes no one. He hates everyone. That's what he is all about.
He hates us. He wants to see us destroyed. He seeks the ruin
of our souls.

Satan is the one who inspires and fuels the Antichrist. But
as he rises to power, the Antichrist will hide his fury well. He
may even appear to be rather loving and a real diplomat. He
may have great political skills. But inwardly he will have the
heart of Satan and be filled with hatred.

It's hard for us to imagine the Antichrist, someone filled
with so much rage. But some of the biblical writers had a
human role model in mind when they wrote about this despi-
cable figure. Both Daniel and the author of 1 and 2 Macabees
(these two books are part of the Apocrypha but are not
included in most Protestant Bibles) believed the prototype

of the Antichrist was Antiochus IV, ruler of Greece's Seleucid Empire. A man of great power and authority, Antiochus adopted the title "Theos Epiphanes," which means "God Manifest." This should have been a warning that even greater ego problems would soon become apparent.

In 169 BC, Antiochus moved his armies south toward Egypt, crossing through Israel, which was under his control. He conquered much of Egypt, but not Alexandria, the capitol. So, he returned in 168 BC to finish the job. This time he was surprised to meet the vastly superior Roman army, which had signed a mutual defense pact with Egypt. Antiochus knew he could not defeat the Roman fighting machine, and he did not want to put Greece in conflict with Rome, so he retreated. As you might expect, this was a huge blow to his ego.

An enraged Antiochus retraced his steps back through Israel. Already hating the Jews, he now let his hatred fuel his actions—slaughtering forty thousand Jewish men, women, and children in the streets of Jerusalem in just three days. He then went into the Jewish temple on the Temple Mount. He desecrated the temple with abominable things and dedicated it to the Greek god Zeus. The Bible calls this "the desolating sacrilege" (Matthew 24:15). The temple was not ritually cleansed until 164, when Judas Maccabeus restored the temple. Jews celebrate this restoration in the festival of Hanukkah.

Even though the story ends happily, the Jews never forgot the insane butchery of Antiochus, who would become a prototype of the Antichrist for future Jewish writers. When Old Testament prophets such as Daniel saw a vision of the end times, and when New Testament writers such as John were given a revelation of the Last Things, they couldn't help but think about the Greek ruler Antiochus, whose hatred and twisted ego led him to commit monstrous acts.

Good Guys and Bad Guys

Portions of Revelation sound like a shootout at the OK Corral. There's a false prophet, who serves as a kind of sidekick to the Antichrist. There's a great harlot, who sits atop Mystery Babylon, symbolic of the theological and moral apostasy of the final days.

But there's also a "good guy" riding into town. This good guy is the restrainer Paul mentions in 2 Thessalonians 2: "You know what is restraining him now so that he may be revealed in his time" (ESV). We don't know exactly what the restrainer does, but somehow he restrains the evil of the age from its full-blown force. Then, one day, the restrainer will be taken out of the way.

Scholars disagree over the identity of the restrainer. Some suggest that the church of Jesus Christ restrains the rise of the Antichrist and limits the power of the spirit of antichrist. I like this interpretation, though I can't prove this is what the Bible means. Still, it's inspiring to think of the impact the church of Jesus Christ has had in our world throughout the ages.

Dr. Gunther Louie is a professor at the University of Massachusetts. He happens to be an atheist, but that didn't stop him from writing a book entitled *Why America Needs Religion*. Louie had planned to write a different book, called *Why America Doesn't Need Religion,* until his research showed that Christians have done some truly wonderful things over the ages. They've built hospitals, schools, and orphanages. They've established ministries that reach out to the poor. They've been involved in social action and fought against oppression. Of course, there have been occasions when Christians were perpetrators of oppression. But Louie saw, for the most part, that Christians have been on the right side of things and have had a positive impact on the world. Though Louie remains an atheist, he does believe that, throughout history, Christianity has been a restrainer—it has made the world a better place and kept evil in check.

The interpretation of the church as the restrainer has some weaknesses. For one thing, some biblical passages call the restrainer "he," but this pronoun is never applied to the church in Scripture.

Another theory is that the restrainer is God-ordained government. This interpretation is probably the most common among biblical scholars, in part because Paul wrote in Romans 13 that governments are instituted by God to deter evil on Earth. Paul further warned that the governing authority "does not bear the sword in vain; he is the servant of God to execute his wrath on the wrongdoer." Under this scenario, when earthly governments cease to effectively restrain wickedness, the Antichrist will arise with the power of full-blown evil.

We Know How the Story Ends

Some baseball buffs get so caught up in the box scores and player statistics that they almost lose sight of which team wins the game. Christians can do the same thing with the end times. They are so focused on the trees—such as the identity of the restrainer, or what 666 means—they lose sight of the forest.

It's important to remember who wins. Christ will emerge triumphant. The Bible says, "And then the lawless one will be revealed, and the Lord Jesus will slay him with the breath of his mouth and destroy him by his appearing and his coming" (2 Thessalonians 2:8). One little word from Jesus will slay the Antichrist. He will be destroyed by Christ's appearing; Christ will prevail.

The power of the Antichrist's hate will be overcome by the power of Christ's splendor and love. To some, that seems a pipe dream. To others, it seems counterintuitive, in part because we have all seen cases of the bad guy winning or of hate seemingly triumphing over love.

But the reality is that love will win over hate. Goodness will triumph over evil. Christ will defeat the Antichrist. And the way we live out the truth of this hope *now* is to love our enemies as Christ said we should. By expressing our faith in such a radical, countercultural manner, we demonstrate our commitment to Christ's ultimate victory over the Antichrist.

In his Sermon on the Plain, Jesus said these things to his disciples.

> But I say to you who hear, Love your enemies, do good to those who hate you, bless those who curse you, pray for those who abuse you. To him who strikes you on the cheek, offer the other also, and from him who takes away your cloak do not withhold your tunic either. Give to every one who begs from you, and from one who takes away your goods do not demand them back. And

as you wish that others would do to you, do so to them.

If you love those who love you, what benefit is that to you? For even sinners love those who love them. And if you do good to those who do good to you, what credit is that to you? For even sinners do the same. And if you lend to those from whom you hope to receive, what credit is that to you? Even sinners lend to sinners, to get back the same amount. But love your enemies, and do good, and lend, expecting nothing in return, and your reward will be great, and you will be sons of the Most High; for he is kind to the ungrateful and the selfish. Be merciful, even as your Father is merciful. Judge not, and you will not be judged; condemn not, and you will not be condemned; forgive, and you will be forgiven; give, and it will be given to you. Good measure, pressed down, shaken together, running over, will be put into your lap. For with the measure you use it will be measured back to you. (Luke 6:27–38 ESV)

I know there are times when this may seem like a fantasy that has no chance of success in our "real" world, where might often makes right. But our real world will not look so real when it begins to disappear and makes way for a more real world planned by God to replace it.

In *that* world, love will be more powerful than hate. Light will be more real than darkness. The Spirit of Christ will be more real than the spirit of antichrist.

If we believe this, let's put that belief into action today. Instead of daydreaming about what things will be like after Christ's ultimate victory, let's begin living as if we believe that love will triumph over hate.

By living this way, we can show through our current actions the faith and hope we have in a glorious time that is sure to come.

— 7 —

THE RAPTURE:

RETURNING TO JUDGE AND REDEEM

World War II created more than its share of larger-than-life heroes, but few were as famous as General Douglas MacArthur, Supreme Allied Commander in the Southwest Pacific. Soon after the United States entered the war, MacArthur led the fight against the Japanese forces that had invaded the Philippine Islands. But the Allied forces were outmanned and suffered a humiliating defeat. When he was reassigned to Australia, MacArthur made a promise to the Filipino people: "I shall return."

For the next two years under Japanese occupation, the Filipino people suffered torture, starvation, and death, and the nation suffered great physical damage. But in the autumn of 1944, MacArthur did return, and with vast armies and great military power. Today, many Filipino people regard MacArthur as a liberator.

Almost two thousand years ago, our Lord Jesus Christ left this earth. He knew that his people would be embattled and outnumbered. He knew they would face struggles and sometimes even torture and death. But he promised that he would return: "Surely I am coming soon" (Revelation 22:20). Now we await the fulfillment of his promise.

People who lived nearly two thousand years ago believed they would see the fulfillment of this promise during their lifetime. And since that time, the hope of seeing Christ return has inspired every generation.

Will our generation be the one that finally welcomes Christ back to Earth? I hope so, but the truth is that I really don't know. One thing is certain. When Jesus does come back to our planet, he will be fulfilling a two-fold purpose for the world. Let's examine what the Bible says Christ will accomplish when he returns.

Coming to Judge the World

Jesus is love incarnate. When he walked this earth, he healed the sick, forgave sinners, and reached out to those whom everyone else ignored or abused. Jesus is God's expression of love for humanity.

But we must remember one thing. When Christ returns to Earth, he will come to judge the nations, as John told us in Revelation 1:7: "Behold, he is coming with the clouds, and every eye will see him, every one who pierced him; and all tribes of the earth will wail on account of Him. Even so. Amen."

Jesus himself said he is coming to judge us: "Behold, I am coming soon, bringing my recompense, to repay every one for what he has done. I am the Alpha and the Omega, the first and the last, the beginning and the end" (Revelation 22:12–13).

This may sound surprising to some, but in fact, Jesus always combined mercy and judgment in his teachings. This passage in Revelation isn't the first time Jesus said he would judge the world. He discussed his second coming in the Olivet Discourse, found in Matthew 24–25.

> When the Son of man comes in his glory, and all the angels with him, then he will sit on his glorious throne. Before him will be gathered all the nations, and he will separate them one from another as a shepherd separates the sheep from the goats, and he will place the sheep at his right hand, but the goats at the left. Then the King will say to those at his right hand, "Come, O blessed of my Father, inherit the kingdom prepared for you from the foundation of the world; for I was hungry and you gave me food, I was thirsty and you gave me drink, I was a stranger and you welcomed me, I was naked and you clothed me, I was sick and you visited me, I was in prison and you came to me." Then the righteous will answer him, "Lord, when did we see thee hungry and feed thee, or thirsty and give thee drink? And when did we see thee a stranger and welcome thee, or naked and clothe thee? And when did we see thee sick or in prison and visit thee?" And the

King will answer them, "Truly, I say to you, as
you did it to one of the least of these my brethren,
you did it to me." Then he will say to those at his
left hand, "Depart from me, you cursed, into the
eternal fire prepared for the devil and his angels;
for I was hungry and you gave me no food, I
was thirsty and you gave me no drink, I was a
stranger and you did not welcome me, naked and
you did not clothe me, sick and in prison and
you did not visit me." Then they also will answer,
"Lord, when did we see thee hungry or thirsty or
a stranger or naked or sick or in prison, and did
not minister to thee?" Then he will answer them,
"Truly, I say to you, as you did it not to one of
the least of these, you did it not to me." And they
will go away into eternal punishment, but the
righteous into eternal life." (25:31–46)

Some of us don't like the concept of judgment, but it's
an important aspect of the righteous character of God, who
created the world and places moral demands on us while we
live here.

Each of us has a choice. In this life, we have the freedom
to obey God's moral demands or to ignore them. If we choose
to obey, we have nothing to fear from divine judgment. The
final judgment, however, will be a much more troubling event
for those who choose to ignore the Creator's moral plan for
his creation.

God's judgment is apparent in many portions of the Old
Testament. The Jews developed many names for God based
on his many attributes. They created names such as *Jehovah-*

Jireh, which means "The Lord Who Provides"; *Jehovah-Nissi,* which means "The Lord Our Victory"; and *Jehovah-Shalom,* which means "The Lord Our Peace." They also referred to God as *Jehovah-Makkeh,* which means "The Lord Who Smites." There was no question in their minds but that the God of peace was also the God of righteous judgment.

Many of us make a distinction between the God of the Old Testament and the God of the New Testament. It's understandable, because in the New Testament, Jesus comes to pronounce the good news and usher in the kingdom of God. He taught that the greatest commandments are to love God and to love our neighbor. He proclaimed the forgiveness of sin and the salvation of the sinner.

But the Jesus of the New Testament is one in nature and purpose with the God of the Old Testament. The loving Jesus who came into Jerusalem on Palm Sunday, meekly riding on a donkey, is the same Jesus who will return at the end of the age, riding a white horse to judge the world. Here is John's description in Revelation 19.

> I saw heaven opened, and behold, a white horse! He who sat upon it is called Faithful and True, and in righteousness he judges and makes war. His eyes are like a flame of fire, and on his head are many diadems; and he has a name inscribed which no one knows but himself. He is clad in a robe dipped in blood, and the name by which he is called is The Word of God. And the armies of heaven, arrayed in fine linen, white and pure, followed him on white horses. From his mouth issues a sharp sword with which to smite the

nations, and he will rule them with a rod of iron; he will tread the wine press of the fury of the wrath of God the Almighty. On his robe and on his thigh he has a name inscribed, King of kings and Lord of lords.

It's true. Jesus was a messenger of God's love, but he will also serve as an enforcer of God's holy judgment on a sinful world. If we fail to recognize this, we see only a partial picture of our Lord and his mission.

Coming to Receive His People

Judgment is the second purpose of Christ's mission when he returns to Earth, but it's not the whole story. He will also come to receive his people to himself.

Many Christians refer to this process as the *rapture*, which means to be "caught up." Here's how Paul describes the rapture in 1 Thessalonians 4.

But we would not have you ignorant, brethren, concerning those who are asleep, that you may not grieve as others do who have no hope. For since we believe that Jesus died and rose again, even so, through Jesus, God will bring with him those who have fallen asleep. For this we declare to you by the word of the Lord, that we who are alive, who are left until the coming of the Lord, shall not precede those who have fallen asleep. The Lord himself will descend from heaven with a cry of command, with the archangel's call, and with the sound of the trumpet of God. And the dead in Christ will rise first; then we who are alive, who are left, shall be caught up together with them in the clouds to meet the Lord in the air; and so we shall always be with the Lord. Therefore comfort one another with these words. (vv. 13–18)

Paul also discussed the rapture in 2 Thessalonians 2:1, where he mentioned "the coming of our Lord Jesus Christ and our assembling to meet him," and in 1 Corinthians 15:51–52, where he wrote, "I tell you a mystery. We shall not all sleep, but we shall all be changed, in a moment, in the twinkling of an eye, at the last trumpet. For the trumpet will sound and the dead will be raised imperishable, and we shall be changed."

When those who are alive are raptured, Jesus will also resurrect the bodies of those Christians who have already died. Their souls will have already left this earth, and their spirits will have already joined with Christ in heaven.

As Paul told us in 1 Thessalonians 4 and other passages, both those who are alive and those who are dead when Christ returns will become clothed in their resurrection bodies. We know little about these resurrected bodies, except for one thing: they are going to be beautiful. Paul wrote more in this wonderful passage in 1 Corinthians 15.

> But some one will ask, "How are the dead raised? With what kind of body do they come?"
>
> You foolish man! What you sow does not come to life unless it dies. And what you sow is not the body which is to be, but a bare kernel, perhaps of wheat or of some other grain. But God

gives it a body as he has chosen, and to each kind
of seed its own body. For not all flesh is alike, but
there is one kind for men, another for animals,
another for birds, and another for fish. There are
celestial bodies and there are terrestrial bodies;
but the glory of the celestial is one, and the glory
of the terrestrial is another. There is one glory
of the sun, and another glory of the moon, and
another glory of the stars; for star differs from star
in glory.

So is it with the resurrection of the dead.
What is sown is perishable, what is raised is
imperishable. It is sown in dishonor, it is raised
in glory. It is sown in weakness, it is raised in
power. It is sown a physical body, it is raised a
spiritual body. If there is a physical body, there is
also a spiritual body. Thus it is written, "The first
man Adam became a living being"; the last Adam
became a life-giving spirit. But it is not the spiritual which is first but the physical, and then the
spiritual. The first man was from the earth, a man
of dust; the second man is from heaven. As was
the man of dust, so are those who are of the dust;
and as is the man of heaven, so are those who are
of heaven. Just as we have borne the image of the
man of dust, we shall also bear the image of the
man of heaven. I tell you this, brethren: flesh and
blood cannot inherit the kingdom of God, nor
does the perishable inherit the imperishable.

Lo! I tell you a mystery. We shall not all sleep,

but we shall all be changed, in a moment, in the twinkling of an eye, at the last trumpet. For the trumpet will sound, and the dead will be raised imperishable, and we shall be changed. For this perishable nature must put on the imperishable, and this mortal nature must put on immortality. When the perishable puts on the imperishable, and the mortal puts on immortality, then shall come to pass the saying that is written: "Death is swallowed up in victory."

"O death, where is thy victory? O death, where is thy sting?"

The sting of death is sin, and the power of sin is the law. But thanks be to God, who gives us the victory through our Lord Jesus Christ.

Therefore, my beloved brethren, be steadfast, immovable, always abounding in the work of the Lord, knowing that in the Lord your labor is not in vain. (1 Corinthians 15:35–58)

What a great passage! Our resurrection bodies will be heavenly, indestructible, incorruptible, and no longer subject to decay.

I don't know about you, but there are times when I look in the mirror and the signs of decay are all too obvious. There are fresh wrinkles in my skin. There are changes in both the color and quantity of my hair. And there are other signs of aging throughout my mind and my body. I'm not dead yet, but I can certainly see the early signs of the decay that afflicts all of us in our earthly bodies.

Our heavenly bodies will not be subject to such decay. Instead, they will be powerful. The New Testament uses the word *dunamis,* from which we get the word *dynamite.* So, if you've ever wanted a dynamite body, you will get one! Our new bodies are "raised in power." They will be *pneumatikos,* which means "governed by the Spirit" rather than governed by the physical laws of the universe, as our bodies currently are.

I love the passage in Psalm 110 that says our new bodies will resemble the freshness of the morning dew. And I particularly like how the Psalmist says our youth will return to us.

The various words biblical writers used to describe our new bodies say these bodies will be

- fit for heaven
- governed by the Spirit
- dynamic
- no longer subject to decay
- worthy of praise

That's exciting. I look forward to the return of Christ, the rapture, and the resurrection of my body.

What Happens When?

All of us are curious about which event will happen when. After all, we schedule activities on our calendars weeks ahead of time. We schedule vacations and holidays. We are planners, and we like to know what's around the next bend.

Unfortunately, the Bible does not give as much information as we might like to have about the Last Things. The passages about the rapture are few, they are typically brief, and they are limited in what they cover. But that hasn't stopped debates, arguments, and even bitterness as believers interpret the various passages in different ways.

Certain groups of Christians seem to be especially anxious about the chronology of events. The Christians in Thessalonica were just such a group. In two separate letters, Paul wrote to calm these worried believers. In one case, he even reminded them that no matter how soon they believe Christ is returning, it's unwise to quit their jobs and lie around waiting for the end of the world. "If any one will not work, let him not eat," Paul told the busybodies in Thessalonica (2 Thessalonians 3:10).

In the 1960s, anxiety about the end of the world was ratcheted up by a number of factors, including the proliferation of atomic weapons that could annihilate life on Earth and the establishment of Israel as a nation. In chapter two, we talked about Hal Lindsey's bestselling book *The Late Great Planet Earth*. That book was published in 1970, a time of widespread concern about the future—both in the church and in U.S. society-at-large. Contemporary Christian songs such as Larry Norman's "I Wish We'd All Been Ready" only added to the excitement and the anxiety of the times.

In the 1990s, Christians had new reasons for thinking about the end times. The popular *Left Behind* novels intrigued many people. But it wasn't just fictional stories that had some people concerned. As we approached the end of the twentieth century and the beginning of the twentieth-first century, some people said the transition from one century to the next would bring a global tragedy known as Y2K. People stored food and water for the worldwide meltdown, an event that never materialized.

Over the centuries, more theories than we can count, much less describe, have been advanced about the rapture and its relationship to the tribulation. But people who study the relevant biblical passages have pretty much sorted themselves into three main camps. Let's look at their views.

Three Major Views of the Rapture

The three major views Christians have developed about how the end times will unfold try to fit the rapture into a scheme that also includes the tribulation (discussed in chapter four). But these views disagree on whether the rapture will happen before, during, or after the tribulation. Although libraries of books have been written about these arguments, these brief summaries that follow cover some of the key points and disagreements of the three main views.

Pre-Tribulation Rapture (Pre-Trib)

Pre-tribulationists believe Christ will rapture (or remove) his followers *before* the final tribulation. Pre-tribulationists (such as John Darby and Hal Lindsey) argue that, since God's divine wrath is not directed toward the church, believers will be removed from the earth before the trials of the tribulation break out.

One key Bible passage used to support this view is 2 Thessalonians 2:6–8: "And you know what restrains him now, so that in his time he may be revealed. For the mystery of lawlessness is already at work; only he who now restrains will do so until he is taken out of the way. And then that lawless one will be revealed whom the Lord will slay with the breath of His mouth and bring to an end by the appearance of

His coming" (NASB). This passage says the one who restrains lawlessness must be removed before the Antichrist can be revealed. This restrainer is believed by pre-tribulationists to be the Holy Spirit, and if he were removed, they argue, those indwelled by him would be removed as well.

Another key passage for this view is Revelation 3:10: "Because you have kept the word of My perseverance, I also will keep you from the hour of testing, that hour which is about to come upon the whole world, to test those who dwell upon the earth" (NASB). Here, Jesus tells the early churches that he will keep them from the hour of trial that is coming on the whole world. Following Jesus' letters to the churches recorded in Revelation 2 and 3, the focus of the book shifts from the church to the nation of Israel for the passages on the tribulation.

Mid-Tribulation Rapture (Mid-Trib)

Mid-tribulationists (such as Harold Ockenga) believe the rapture will take place in the middle of the tribulation period. The key Bible passages mid-tribulationists point to are Daniel 7, 9, and 12, and Revelation 11 and 12. These passages refer to a period of forty-two months, or three and one-half years, which is half of the seven-year tribulation period. Christians will suffer somewhat during the first three and one-half years, but then will be raptured before the full fury of God's wrath is poured out on the rest of the world.

This view says that because the church was promised tribulation (John 15:18–19; 16:33), it can expect to experience the first half of the tribulation period. Mid-tribulationists often cite Acts 14:22 and Romans 12:12, which refer to actual persecution of the saints, as a preview or partial fulfillment of the tribulation to come.

Post-Tribulation Rapture (Post-Trib)

Post-tribulationists (such as Wayne Grudem) believe the rapture will take place at the end of the tribulation, which means Christians will endure all the horrors of the entire tribulation period. Defenders of this position point to Jesus' words in the Olivet Discourse, recorded in Matthew 24–25.

> Immediately after the tribulation of those days the sun will be darkened, and the moon will not give its light, and the stars will fall from heaven, and the powers of the heavens will be shaken; then will appear the sign of the Son of Man in heaven, and then all the tribes of the earth will mourn, and they will see the Son of man coming on the clouds of heaven with power and great glory; and he will send out his angels with a loud trumpet call, and they will gather his elect from the four winds, from one end of heaven to the other. (24:29–31)

Post-tribulationists argue that these passages, and many others that instruct believers in how to survive the tribulation, make no sense unless believers are present throughout the entire tribulation period. Post-tribulationists also argue that the other views are based on questionable assumptions about which biblical passages refer to the church and which refer to Israel.

Wrestling with the Three Major Views of the Rapture

Obviously, each of these three positions has some merits. Otherwise, people would not commit themselves to a particular view. Which position makes the most sense to you? If you've been in churches where one view is promoted and the others are dismissed, your position may be based only on the fact that you're unfamiliar with the other positions.

If I had my choice, I would prefer the pre-tribulationist view. That's because I believe the tribulation will be very difficult, and I would prefer that the church not have to endure its horrors. But God is not going to base the end of the world on my preferences. And no matter how strongly and eloquently representatives of each position defend their views, two of these views will be found to be wrong.

Many members of our church have asked me to state my position in a definitive way, but I've refused to do so. It's not that I'm trying to be coy. I am merely trying to be faithful to all of the biblical passages that explore issues of the rapture.

I don't believe the Bible is clear on this issue. Each view has biblical passages that appear to support it. For thirty-five years, I've studied these things, and I can defend all three positions. But in my view, none summarizes *all* of the passages.

Some people expect pastors to lay down the law, in back and white terms, even when the reality of the situation contains shades of gray. In part, that's because people face many choices today, and they want trustworthy authorities to help them make some of those choices.

There are also people who believe that leaders need to favor one side or another in every argument. If they don't do so, they're labeled as soft or indecisive.

I'm neither soft nor indecisive, and I have no problem committing myself to a position—when I am sure that the Bible is clear one way or the other. I'm willing to stake my life on those things God has clearly revealed in Scripture.

But when I feel God's Word is unclear or ambiguous on a particular point, I feel that I need to remain ambiguous, to withhold judgment, to acknowledge that I don't know everything. That's the predicament I find myself in after years of studying the rapture. The Bible does not give the clarity and assurance I need to claim understanding of God's truth on the matter.

In the famous "love" chapter, 1 Corinthians 13, Paul wrote, "For now we see only a reflection as in a mirror; then we shall see face to face. Now I know in part; then I shall know fully, even as I am fully known" (v. 13 TNIV). For now, our knowledge about Last Things is incomplete.

But we do know two important things with certainty. Jesus is coming to judge the nations, and he will receive his people unto himself. So for me, the focus should be on preparing our minds and hearts for this eventuality rather than fighting over the specific game plan God will use to get it all done.

Millions of people who have read the *Left Behind* books, or the books by Hal Lindsey, have been persuaded to adopt the pre-tribulationist view. But I don't believe we should be persuaded by novels or movies to adopt one position before we've studied the alternatives. Unfortunately, there are no bestselling books persuasively arguing for the other positions on the tribulation. I urge you to hold loosely to your certainties concerning the three competing views of the rapture, because the Bible seems unclear on this point.

Meanwhile, hold steadfastly to the things about which the Bible is clear, including a number of teachings about the judgment we will now examine.

Judgment Starts with Us

Sometimes people talk about God's judgment using the terms *us* and *them*. Their language reveals that they're convinced *we* (which could mean everybody in their church, their family, or their circle of loved ones) are destined for nothing but good things, while *they* (everybody else) are destined to eternal torment and punishment. I typically want to say, "Wait a minute. It's not just the world that's going to be judged. We who believe in Jesus Christ are going to be judged too!"

This judgment will be different from the eternal judgment that determines who goes to heaven and who goes to hell. Still, Paul made it clear in 1 Corinthians 3:10–15 that followers of Jesus will be judged.

> By the grace God has given me, I laid a foundation as a wise builder, and someone else is building on it. But each one should build with care. For no one can lay any foundation other than the one already laid, which is Jesus Christ. If anyone builds on this foundation using gold, silver, costly stones, wood, hay or straw, their work will be shown for what it is, because the Day will bring it to light. It will be revealed with fire, and the fire will test the quality of each person's work. If what has been built survives, the builder will receive a reward. If it is burned up, the builder will suffer

loss but yet will be saved—even though only as one escaping through the flames. (TNIV)

Our lives will be tested. If we've built our lives on the foundation of Jesus Christ, we will be safe. Paul also said some of us will be saved, but "only as one escaping through the flames." For these people, heaven awaits, but there will be no escaping the odor of smoke. That's something we should all consider.

Some people believe that all Christians will enjoy the same rewards in heaven. But most Bible scholars reject this concept of a one-size-fits-all afterlife. Many passages make it clear that our rewards will vary. Of course, thanks to God's grace, we will all receive much better than we deserve. Still, it seems clear that God has chosen to reward his people based on their faithfulness in this life. Our lives will be tested and weighed in the balance.

I believe one factor that will weigh heavily in this judgment is how we have related to Christ's body on Earth, his church. Jesus said that he would "build his church and the powers of Hades, the gates of hell, would not prevail against it" (Matthew 16:18 ESV).

In 1 Corinthians 3:16–17, Paul talked about the afterlife: "Do you not know that you are God's temple and that God's Spirit dwells in you? If anyone destroys God's temple, God will destroy him. For God's temple is holy and that temple you are."

So, what was Paul talking about? Many say this passage is about taking care of our physical bodies and not destroying them with bad habits. But I believe Paul was talking about the church. He was speaking to us not individually, but collectively, as Christ's body. Paul was warning us against destroying Christ's church.

That's why I ask this important question. How's it going with you and the church? I know the church has flaws. But what are you doing to love and serve this flawed institution that is Christ's body? Maybe you see how corrupt and sinful people in the church can be. But are you ignoring the fact that you too have problems?

Do you attend a church in your area? Do you give your time, talents, and abilities to the service of a local congregation? Do you pray for your church and for the worldwide body of Christ? Do you give your treasure to the work and ministry of your church?

Movie director Woody Allen once said, "I don't want to be a member of any organization that would accept someone like me as a member." Some may feel the same way about church.

But Christ came to Earth to save sinners. That means you and me. Every week, forgiven sinners gather in churches around the globe to thank God for his mercy and to learn how they can better walk in the footsteps of Jesus.

As church people, we aren't perfect, but we're on a journey to God. We ask you to join us so that we can help each other grow into the likeness of Christ.

Surpassing Beauty

When some people imagine the end times, they see only images of fire and chaos and judgment, which are part of the story. But they are only a part. That's why I close this chapter with a beautiful image of the end times from the prophet

Isaiah. In Isaiah 11, the prophet painted a picture of what will happen when Christ returns.

> And his delight shall be in the fear of the LORD. He shall not judge by what his eyes see, or decide by what his ears hear; but with righteousness he shall judge the poor, and decide with equity for the meek of the earth; and he shall smite the earth with the rod of his mouth, and with the breath of his lips he shall slay the wicked. Righteousness shall be the girdle of his waist, and faithfulness the girdle of his loins. The wolf shall dwell with the lamb, and the leopard shall lie down with the kid, and the calf and the lion and the fatling together, and a little child shall lead them. The cow and the bear shall feed; their young shall lie down together; and the lion shall eat straw like the ox. The sucking child shall play over the hole of the asp, and the weaned child shall put his hand on the adder's den. They shall not hurt or destroy in all my holy mountain; for the earth shall be full of the knowledge of the LORD as the waters cover the sea. In that day the root of Jesse shall stand as an ensign to the peoples; him shall the nations seek, and his dwellings shall be glorious. (Isaiah 11:3–10)

Some preachers believe that stories about the flames of hell will scare the hell out of people. In other words, frightening stories about suffering and hell are supposed to manipulate people to turn away from sin and follow God. Maybe that works with some folks. But the best choices are made out of love, not fear. I prefer to paint a beautiful picture of the glories of heaven, in hopes that this image will draw people to a deeper love of God. Both images are true. There's a beautiful story about the glories of heaven. And there's a scary story about the suffering of hell. It's up to you which story you focus on.

I invite you to join me on a journey in this life that will lead to a world beyond our world, where the leopard shall lie down with the kid. Don't you want to live forever with Jesus in that place?

— 8 —

A GUIDED TOUR OF HELL

None of us really wants to go there, but many of us have spent significant amounts of time thinking about hell. Devils and demons have been regular figures in classical literature and popular movies since the time of Dante, who wrote the *Divine Comedy* in the early 1300s. In that epic poem, the ancient Roman poet Virgil leads Dante on a guided tour through hell so that Dante will be freed of the temptation to sin.

C. S. Lewis took readers to hell in his short and surprisingly humorous little book, *The Great Divorce*. In the book, a group of English men and women take a one-day bus trip to hell, where they meet a series of people whose bondages to various sins while alive sealed their eternal fates.

More recently, the movie *What Dreams May Come* gave viewers fascinating views of both heaven and hell. In the movie, Robin Williams plays Chris Nielsen, a man who dies and goes to "Summerland," but journeys to hell to secure the soul of his wife. When Chris is escorted to the gateway of hell, he sees a huge field opening before him. Instead of being covered with grass or plants, the field is full of upturned human faces, crying out with the various temptations and sorrows that afflicted them in life.

While Dante and Lewis based their visions of hell on the Bible, the makers of *What Dreams May Come* based their depiction on New Age and paranormal beliefs. Today, most people try to avoid thinking about hell, but when they do, their ideas are a mishmash of Christian beliefs and other concepts.

In this chapter, we'll tour the key biblical teachings on hell. While it won't be a joyride, I'm convinced that the more we know about the afterlife, including hell, the less confused we'll be. Followers of Christ need not worry about their own eternal destinies. But perhaps this tour will encourage us to reach out to friends or loved ones who aren't quite so certain where they will spend the afterlife.

Major Views of Hell

Christians over the centuries have studied the many biblical passages about hell. Their conclusions drawn from these passages have crystallized into four major views: hell is (1) a place of annihilation, (2) a workhouse on the way to heaven, (3) a place of eternal punishment, and (4) a place where God is not. Let's look at each of these views.

Hell, a Place of Annihilation

The word *annihilation* comes from the Latin *nihil*, which means "nothing." Annihilationists believe souls that go to hell become nothing after a finite period of punishment. In other words, you do your time and you go away.

Some believe that people may go to hell for just a few weeks if they hadn't been very bad. Those more committed to sin and evil while alive may go to hell for a thousand years, experiencing the punitive nature of hell followed by annihilation and the ultimate loss of being. Some Christians have even adopted an annihilationist view of hell because it seems more merciful than believing that God would condemn people to eternal punishment.

I sympathize with their desire to be merciful, but I find no biblical support for any view that suggests people will be in hell or heaven for anything less than eternity. So while support for this view is growing in some Christian circles, I feel annihilationism doesn't consider the greatest number of biblical passages about hell.

Hell, a Workhouse on the Way to Heaven

A second major view sees hell as a place where people atone for their sins. The concept is similar to earlier understandings of crime and punishment. Beginning in the 1600s, criminals were sent to workhouses, where it was believed that sweat and hard work would purify their souls and prepare them to reenter society.

Many Christians who see hell as a workhouse believe that all human souls will eventually find their way to heaven. According to this view, salvation will be universal. Some universalists don't believe in hell at all, and they consider eternal punishment a concept that might be appropriate for small, primitive minds but not for contemporary people, and not for a contemporary God.

Other universalists believe in hell, but they don't believe anyone stays there for eternity. Their view is that hell is temporary and remedial. When sinful or evil people die, they may go to hell for varying lengths of time. The purpose of their time in hell is essentially to make them fit for heaven, where they will find themselves in the presence of God.

Christian universalists look to a number of biblical passages for support, including Ephesians 4 and 1 Peter 3, which they claim reveal that God will indeed take people from hell and put them in heaven.

> Therefore it is said, "When he ascended on high he led a host of captives, and he gave gifts to men." (In saying, "He ascended," what does it mean but that he had also descended into the lower parts of the earth? He who descended is he who also ascended far above all the heavens, that he might fill all things.) (Ephesians 4:8–10)

> For Christ also died for sins once for all, the righteous for the unrighteous, that he might bring us to God, being put to death in the flesh but made alive in the spirit; in which he went and preached to the spirits in prison, who formerly did not obey, when God's patience waited in the days of Noah, during the building of the ark, in which a few, that is, eight persons, were saved through water. Baptism, which corresponds to this, now saves you, not as a removal of dirt from the body but as an appeal to God for a clear conscience, through the resurrection of Jesus Christ, who has gone into heaven and is at the right hand of God,

with angels, authorities, and powers subject to him. (1 Peter 3:18–22)

In Ephesians, we're told that Jesus both ascended to heaven and descended into the lower parts of the earth, leading a host of captives on high with him. A very difficult passage in 1 Peter 3 tells us that during the three-day period between his death and resurrection, Jesus traveled in his spirit and preached to the spirits of those who disobeyed in the days of Noah, when God brought a great deluge on the earth in judgment. Both of these passages have challenged scholars for centuries, but I think it's important to point out that neither passage says Jesus went into hell.

To the original audience of the New Testament, Hades represented a place of the dead. But that is not the same thing as the biblical hell. When people die who do not belong to Jesus Christ, they go to a place where they await the final judgment. This is not hell. No one is in hell yet. Hades has been understood as the place of waiting, and these passages tell us that Jesus went there and did something we don't fully understand. But wherever he went and whatever he did, he did not go to hell and endorse universalism.

Universalists also look to 1 Corinthians 15:22, where Paul wrote, "As in Adam all die, so also in Christ shall all be made alive." Universalists argue that all die in Adam and all live in Christ. But the passage says *all who are in Christ* shall live—*not everyone.*

Other passages present problems for the universalist view. The Bible does not portray hell as a workhouse. Some of the biblical words for hell mean "destruction" or "ruin." These are not remedial words. They describe punishment, not repair.

Nor does the Bible describe hell as temporary. The biblical words for hell convey that it is "eternal," "never-ending," and a "world without end."

God opposes sin, and he judges people who do not turn to Jesus for forgiveness. God does not drag people to heaven or hell who have not already chosen an eternal destiny. He does not sentence us to a term in a workhouse until we see the light. He gives us plenty of time to come to our senses about heaven and hell in *this* life.

Hell, a Place of Eternal Punishment

Having introduced you to two flawed perspectives on hell, it's only fair to introduce you to the view that has been embraced by many Christians ever since the time of Christ. The orthodox and traditional view of hell is that it is punitive and never-ending. I know this is a hard view to appreciate, and it's not the view I would have chosen if it were up to me. But it's not up to me, and I believe it is the only viable view for Christians who are committed to taking God's Word at face value.

We've all heard people ask, "If God is love, how could he send people to hell?" Maybe some of us even ask that question ourselves at times. But we need to remember that God doesn't *send* people to hell. He only judges them. It's what he sees when he renders that judgment that determines where we spend eternity.

In the Bible, there are a variety of images of hell. Revelation 19, 20, and 21 call hell "a lake of fire." Other passages in Revelation speak of people being sentenced to the "bottomless pit." Jesus often spoke of hell as "the outer darkness." In the parable of talents, Jesus said to "cast the worthless servant into the outer darkness; there men will weep and gnash their teeth" (Matthew 25:30).

Jesus also taught an image of hell that was based on a garbage dump located in the Hinnom Valley, outside of Jerusalem. When Jesus called hell "gehenna," he referenced this Hinnom Valley dump, a burning pile of trash that had been building up for centuries.

None of the Bible's various images of hell are meant to be taken literally. In other words, biblical writers used imagery and imaginative language to paint a picture of something they didn't completely understand. But one common theme is suffering. If there's one thing we know about hell, it will involve suffering.

In 2 Thessalonians 1:7–9, Paul told us, "The Lord Jesus is revealed from heaven with his mighty angels in flaming fire, inflicting vengeance upon those who do not know God and upon those who do not obey the gospel of our Lord Jesus. They shall suffer the punishment of eternal destruction and exclusion from the presence of the Lord and from the glory of his might."

Hell, a Place Where God Is Not

God is not in hell torturing people, because God is not in hell. As Paul said in the verse we just looked at, those who do not obey the gospel shall suffer "exclusion from the presence of the Lord and from the glory of His might." God will not be in hell, which is the primary cause of the suffering that will be experienced there. God's divine absence will be a source of anguish and suffering.

I know this can be difficult to harmonize with the doctrine of God's omnipresence, which says that God is everywhere. But hell is the one exception to this doctrine. It's the one place where God is not to be found. That, in itself, is what makes hell so hellish.

Sometimes we forget that God is everywhere present. There is no place in this world where even the most entrenched atheist does not benefit from the loving compassion of our Father. The atheist does not realize this, of course. Yet it's true. No one in this world is completely miserable, because God is everywhere. The Bible says that all joy comes from God. In fact, all good things come from God. "In thy presence there is fullness of joy, in thy right hand are pleasures for evermore" (Psalm 16:11).

Suffering in hell is so intense, in part, because it involves the absence of God, which is a condition no one in this life has ever experienced. In a sense, this absence of God is appropriate, for people who find themselves in hell wanted to live for themselves and without God. God will grant them that wish throughout eternity.

In 2 Timothy 3:1–13, Paul wrote of fallen humanity in the *last times.*

> In the last days there will come times of stress. For men will be lovers of self, lovers of money, proud, arrogant, abusive, disobedient to their parents, ungrateful, unholy, inhuman, implacable, slanderers, profligates, fierce, haters of good, treacherous, reckless, swollen with conceit, lovers of pleasure rather than lovers of God, holding

the form of religion but denying the power of it. Avoid such people. For among them are those who make their way into households and capture weak women, burdened with sins and swayed by various impulses, who will listen to anybody and can never arrive at a knowledge of the truth. As Jannes and Jambres opposed Moses, so these men also oppose the truth, men of corrupt mind and counterfeit faith; but they will not get very far, for their folly will be plain to all, as was that of those two men. Now you have observed my teaching, my conduct, my aim in life, my faith, my patience, my love, my steadfastness, my persecutions, my sufferings, what befell me at Antioch, at Iconium, and at Lystra, what persecutions I endured; yet from them all the Lord rescued me. Indeed all who desire to live a godly life in Christ Jesus will be persecuted, while evil men and impostors will go on from bad to worse, deceivers and deceived.

The Bible teaches that such people will continue being utterly self-sufficient until they wind up in hell, where the naked, solitary self is all they have left.

God's absence from hell is dictated by the fact that he cannot dwell together with sin and evil. Because of his love for us, he allows us to choose our own eternal destiny. But people who choose to live in complete opposition to his will during *this* life, will suffer the consequences of that choice in the *next* life.

Mysteries beyond Comprehension

Whenever I teach on the afterlife, many of our church members, understandably, grow concerned about the status of people they know and love. As we look at some of their chief questions and concerns, I want you to know that my responses are only partial. There is so much more I want to know and understand. But not until I experience the afterlife myself will I even begin to understand some of these profound mysteries of God.

Are There Various Levels of Hell?

People wonder if there are various levels of pain or suffering in hell. Dante certainly thought so. His epic poem *Inferno* describes nine circles of hell, a layered hell. Michelangelo's famous painting *The Last Judgment* also presents a layered picture of hell.

Historically, Christians have believed that hell will be different for different people, in part because not all sins are created equal, so neither are all punishments. Revelation 20 says that people will be judged according to what they have done.

> Then I saw a great white throne and Him who sat upon it, from whose presence earth and heaven fled away, and no place was found for them. And I saw the dead, the great and the small, standing before the throne, and books were opened; and another book was opened, which is the book of life; and the dead were judged from the things which were written in the books, according to their deeds. And the sea gave up the dead which

were in it, and death and Hades gave up the dead which were in them; and they were judged, every one of them according to their deeds. Then death and Hades were thrown into the lake of fire. This is the second death, the lake of fire. And if anyone's name was not found written in the book of life, he was thrown into the lake of fire. (Revelation 20:11–15 NASB)

And in Matthew 11, Jesus said it will be more bearable for some on the day of judgment than for others. God is perfectly just, which means everybody will receive only the punishment they deserve.

Are There States or Conditions between Heaven and Hell?

For many centuries, the Catholic and Orthodox traditions have taught the doctrine of limbo, from the Latin *limbus,* which means "edge" or "border." Limbo was the place where unbaptized infants and children went after death. Some taught that adults could also be in limbo. But Catholic doctrine official Cardinal Joseph Ratzinger, who was named Pope Benedict XVI in 2005, described the theology of limbo as only a theological hypothesis and never a defined truth of faith (http://www.fatima.org/news/newsviews/limbo.asp).

In recent years, the Catholic Church also clarified its teaching on purgatory. For a long time, purgatory was believed to be a place between heaven and hell where people could work out their salvation after death. But the church now teaches that purgatory is a place where heaven-bound people are completely sanctified before they go into the full glories of eternity with God.

Purgatory has never been a Protestant doctrine. We believe that Jesus paid the full penalty for our sins and that when Christians die, they go immediately into the presence of the Lord. We base this belief on scriptures such as 2 Corinthians 5, where Paul talked about being away from his body and being present with the Lord.

> For we know that if the earthly tent we live in is destroyed, we have a building from God, a house not made with hands, eternal in the heavens. Here indeed we groan, and long to put on our heavenly dwelling, so that by putting it on we may not be found naked. For while we are still in this tent, we sigh with anxiety; not that we would be unclothed, but that we would be further clothed, so that what is mortal may be swallowed up by life. He who has prepared us for this very thing is God, who has given us the Spirit as a guarantee. So we are always of good courage; we know that while we are at home in the body we are away from the Lord, for we walk by faith, not by sight. We are of good courage, and we would rather be away from the body and at home with the Lord. So whether we are at home or away, we make it our aim to please him. For we must all appear before the judgment seat of Christ, so that each one may receive good or evil, according to what he has done in the body. (2 Corinthians 5:1–10)

There is no mention in the New Testament of an intermediary state.

What Will Happen to Non-Christians?

This is the big one, isn't it? I think the Bible is clear. People who reject Christ during their lives are lost. Jesus referred to blasphemy of the Holy Spirit in Luke 12 and Mark 3. In John 16:14, Jesus said that the Holy Spirit bears witness about Jesus. I believe those who close their minds and hearts to this witness blaspheme the Holy Spirit by rejecting Christ. And those who do so will suffer the judgment of God.

Of course, there are people who have not heard of Christ. They may live in other nations and cultures where the gospel is not proclaimed. And there are some who may have never really understood the gospel. I run into them all the time. I talk to them in my office.

So, what happens to these people? In Romans 2, Paul said that God will judge the secrets of their hearts by Christ Jesus and their conscience will accuse or perhaps excuse them in that day.

> All who have sinned without the law will also perish without the law, and all who have sinned under the law will be judged by the law. For it is not the hearers of the law who are righteous before God, but the doers of the law who will be justified. When Gentiles who have not the law do by nature what the law requires, they are a law to themselves, even though they do not have the law. They show that what the law requires is written on their hearts, while their conscience

also bears witness and their conflicting thoughts accuse or perhaps excuse them on that day when, according to my gospel, God judges the secrets of men by Christ Jesus. (Romans 2:12–16)

We don't know exactly what that means. But here's a way to look at these issues. Those who know Jesus Christ and have given their lives to him truly are saved. Those who reject Christ truly are lost. For everyone else, we are not to judge. It's in the Lord's hands.

An Eternity for You

One of the most amazing TV shows in history was *The Twilight Zone*. In one episode, a man who is running from the police jumps into a big tube and falls down, down, down into a big room with no exits. There, he's forced to view a family's vacation photos for all of eternity. That's certainly one image of hell.

Another image of hell came to me as my wife, Barb, and I locked ourselves out of the condominium where we were staying during a vacation. We were in the middle of nowhere, in the mountains of western Colorado, with absolutely no one around. We tried everything we could to gain entrance. We jiggled doors and examined windows. I even climbed a pine tree to see if I could reach a third-floor deck. But the higher I climbed, the thinner the tree branches got. Before long, I felt as if I were riding a rubber band instead of climbing a tree. We were outside looking in, and there was nothing we could do about it.

But then an amazing thing happened. We saw a woman walking down the hill in our direction. The closer she got, the more we could see her sweet face and nice smile, and the more she could see our anxiety and frustration. To make a long story short, she was the house cleaner. In five seconds, she used her key to unlock the door, and she let us in.

In the opening chapter of Revelation, Jesus appears to John on the Island of Patmos. Jesus has risen from the grave, his voice is like the sound of many waters, and his face is like the sun shining at full strength. John falls down before him. Jesus touches John and says, "Fear not. . . . I have the keys of Death and Hades."

That's my message to you. Fear not. Jesus has the keys to eternity. All we need to do to gain entry into heaven is to ask the person who holds the keys. We need to know him and love him and serve him. Then the doors to heaven will be opened to us, and the doors to hell will be forever closed.

$$— 9 —$$

A NEW HEAVEN AND
A NEW EARTH

In the last chapter, we took a guided tour of hell. Thankfully, we now turn our attention to heaven, a much more inspiring subject. Just as we examined hell in detail, so we'll also look at heaven, with all of its beauty and all of its complexity. As with many passages about hell, biblical writers also used familiar words or phrases to help us grasp mysteries of heaven we can't fully understand. They're telling us, "Hey, if you understand X, try to imagine Z!"

The New Jerusalem

Looking through God's Word for information and insight into heaven, we find some amazing passages in Hebrews 11–13 that discuss the "New Jerusalem." We all know a little about the physical city of Jerusalem located in Israel. Some of us have had the opportunity to visit there. For thousands of years, this city has been a focus of God's work in our world.

In Hebrews, a book written primarily to Jewish converts to Christianity, we learn about a Jerusalem that will not be located on this earth. Hebrews says the New Jerusalem is a city whose builder and maker is God. Abraham and the patriarchs longed for the day when they could see this heavenly city. We who belong to Jesus Christ are also to seek the New Jerusalem, which has been prepared for God's people.

Revelation 21 and 22 give great insights into the New Jerusalem, with some of the most common and popular images of heaven, such as streets of gold and gates of pearl. This heavenly city is massive, stretching for 1,500 miles in each of four directions. Somehow, its size doesn't stop it from descending to Earth. It will pass through the second heaven, outer space, and enter the first heaven, Earth's atmosphere.

In this city are three special groups of beings, according to Hebrews 12. The first is innumerable angels in festal gathering. That's a powerful image: countless angels dressed up for various festivities. The second group in the celestial city is the assembly of the first-born enrolled in the heavens, that is, millions upon millions who've been part of Christ's spiritual body—the church—since the time of Christ. All who have joined themselves to Christ by embracing him and serving him are enrolled in the heavens, because their names are written in the Lamb's book of life (Revelation 21:27).

The third group is the spirits of just men and women who have been made perfect. Who is this group? No one knows. Many suggest these are people who followed God without knowing of Christ, for example, natives of North America who somehow reached out to the Living God before Europeans arrived and preached the gospel. Others believe this group refers to Old Testament saints. That seems reasonable. If this is the case, I will enjoy the opportunity to sit down and talk with Abraham, Moses, Sarah, Rebekah, Rachel, and some of the other people who loved God before the time of Christ.

These three groups will live in the New Jerusalem. The following passage from John's Revelation paints a glorious picture of what life there will be like.

> Then I saw a new heaven and a new earth; for the first heaven and the first earth had passed away, and the sea was no more. And I saw the holy city, new Jerusalem, coming down out of heaven from God, prepared as a bride adorned for her husband; and I heard a loud voice from the throne saying, "Behold, the dwelling of God is with men. He will dwell with them, and they shall be his people, and God himself will be with them; he will wipe away every tear from their eyes, and death shall be no more, neither shall there be mourning nor crying nor pain any more, for the former things have passed away."
>
> And he who sat upon the throne said, "Behold, I make all things new." Also he said, "Write this, for these words are trustworthy and true." And he said to me, "It is done! I am the Alpha and the Omega, the beginning and the end. To the thirsty I will give from the fountain of the water of life without payment. He who conquers shall have this heritage, and I will be his

God and he shall be my son. But as for the cowardly, the faithless, the polluted, as for murderers, fornicators, sorcerers, idolaters, and all liars, their lot shall be in the lake that burns with fire and sulphur, which is the second death."

Then came one of the seven angels who had the seven bowls full of the seven last plagues, and spoke to me, saying, "Come, I will show you the Bride, the wife of the Lamb." And in the Spirit he carried me away to a great, high mountain, and showed me the holy city Jerusalem coming down out of heaven from God, having the glory of God, its radiance like a most rare jewel, like a jasper, clear as crystal. It had a great, high wall, with twelve gates, and at the gates twelve angels, and on the gates the names of the twelve tribes of the sons of Israel were inscribed; on the east three gates, on the north three gates, on the south three gates, and on the west three gates. And the wall of the city had twelve foundations, and on them the twelve names of the twelve apostles of the Lamb.

And he who talked to me had a measuring rod of gold to measure the city and its gates and walls. The city lies foursquare, its length the same as its breadth; and he measured the city with his rod, twelve thousand stadia; its length and breadth and height are equal. He also measured its wall, a hundred and forty-four cubits by a man's measure, that is, an angel's. The wall was built of jasper, while the city was pure gold, clear as glass. The foundations of the wall of the city were adorned with every jewel; the first was jasper, the second sapphire, the third agate, the fourth emerald, the fifth onyx, the sixth carnelian, the seventh chrysolite, the eighth beryl, the ninth topaz, the tenth chrysoprase, the eleventh jacinth, the twelfth amethyst. And the twelve gates were twelve pearls, each of the gates made of a single pearl, and the street of the city was pure gold, transparent as glass.

And I saw no temple in the city, for its temple is the Lord God the Almighty and the Lamb. And the city has no need of sun or moon to shine upon it, for the glory of God is its light, and its lamp is the Lamb. By its light shall the nations walk; and the kings of the earth shall bring their glory into it, and its gates shall never be shut by day—and there shall be no night there; they shall bring into it the glory and the honor of the nations. But nothing unclean shall enter it, nor any one who practices abomination or falsehood, but only those who are written in the Lamb's book of life.

Then he showed me the river of the water of life, bright as crystal, flowing from the throne of God and of the Lamb through the middle of the street of the city; also, on either side of the river, the tree of life with its twelve kinds of fruit, yielding its fruit each month; and the leaves of the tree were for the healing of the nations.

There shall no more be anything accursed, but
the throne of God and of the Lamb shall be in it,
and his servants shall worship him; they shall see
his face, and his name shall be on their foreheads.
And night shall be no more; they need no light of
lamp or sun, for the Lord God will be their light,
and they shall reign for ever and ever. (Revelation
21:1–22:5)

This beautiful image of the New Jerusalem uses metaphorical language to describe the church as the bride of Christ
and the wife of the Lamb.

We also see that the city is built on the foundation of the
twelve apostles and is a temple for the Lord God Almighty
and the Lamb, who is Jesus. In the city, there is a tree of life
(a symbol of eternal life) and the water of life (a symbol of the
Holy Spirit).

Much of this language is metaphorical and symbolic.
But that doesn't mean it isn't real. In fact, the New Jerusalem
is more real than anything we have ever seen or known in
this life. Yes, much of the language is mysterious and hard to
grasp. But that doesn't decrease my desire to be there as soon
as God wills it. Like saints throughout the ages, I long for the
day when I can live in this heavenly city.

Exactly when this will happen is a disputed subject. We'll
look at the timing of these events in the rest of this chapter.

A Glorious Thousand-Year Reign

I've preached many sermons on heaven and hell but very few
on the millennium (the English word comes from Latin words
for "thousand" and "year"). That's because the millennium is

so complicated. We know from Revelation 20:1–10 that for a thousand years Jesus Christ will reign on Earth.

> Then I saw an angel coming down from heaven, holding in his hand the key of the bottomless pit and a great chain. And he seized the dragon, that ancient serpent, who is the Devil and Satan, and bound him for a thousand years, and threw him into the pit, and shut it and sealed it over him, that he should deceive the nations no more, till the thousand years were ended. After that he must be loosed for a little while.
>
> Then I saw thrones, and seated on them were those to whom judgment was committed. Also I saw the souls of those who had been beheaded for their testimony to Jesus and for the word of God, and who had not worshiped the beast or its image and had not received its mark on their foreheads or their hands. They came to life, and reigned with Christ a thousand years. The rest of the dead did not come to life until the thousand years were ended. This is the first resurrection. Blessed and holy is he who shares in the first resurrection! Over such the second death has no power, but they shall be priests of God and of Christ, and they shall reign with him a thousand years.
>
> And when the thousand years are ended, Satan will be loosed from his prison and will come out to deceive the nations which are at the four corners of the earth, that is, Gog and

Magog, to gather them for battle; their number
is like the sand of the sea. And they marched up
over the broad earth and surrounded the camp
of the saints and the beloved city; but fire came
down from heaven and consumed them, and the
devil who had deceived them was thrown into the
lake of fire and sulphur where the beast and the
false prophet were, and they will be tormented
day and night for ever and ever.

Other passages tell of the wonderful things that will happen during this period. For one thing, God will fulfill all of the biblical prophecies and promises he made to Israel, such as those found in Isaiah 66:10–27. Israel will become the glory of the nations and the Davidic line will be reestablished in Jerusalem.

Also, during the millennium, we'll see nature restored. It's hard to imagine what God will do in this world when nature is restored and even the animal world is brought into harmony. Of course today, the animal world is at war. Animals eat other animals; every animal has its place in the food chain. Humans have harmed the earth through careless consumption and improper waste disposal, but things will change when God restores nature.

Perhaps that's what the prophet Isaiah described when he wrote the following:

The wolf shall dwell with the lamb, and the leopard shall lie down with the kid, and the calf and
the lion and the fatling together, and a little child
shall lead them. The cow and the bear shall feed;
their young shall lie down together; and the lion

shall eat straw like the ox. The sucking child shall play over the hole of the asp, and the weaned child shall put his hand on the adder's den. They shall not hurt or destroy in all my holy mountain; for the earth shall be full of the knowledge of the LORD as the waters cover the sea. (Isaiah 11:6–9)

To us, this is a powerful millennial picture of nature restored, particularly after hearing reports about environmental degradation and global warming. In fact, Romans 8 says the entire creation waits with eager longing for the revealing of the children of God, because nature itself longs to be set free from its bondage to decay. So, the entire cosmic order is going to be changed.

Isaiah 11 gives us a prophetic insight into Jesus and his work.

A shoot will come up from the stump of Jesse; from his roots a Branch will bear fruit. The Spirit of the LORD will rest on him—the Spirit of wisdom and of understanding, the Spirit of counsel and of might, the Spirit of the knowledge and fear of the LORD—and he will delight in the fear of the LORD. He will not judge by what he sees with his eyes, or decide by what he hears with his ears; but with righteousness he will judge the needy, with justice he will give decisions for the poor of the earth. He will strike the earth with the rod of his mouth; with the breath of his lips he will slay the wicked. Righteousness will be his belt and faithfulness the sash around his waist. (Isaiah 11:1–5 TNIV)

During the millennium, Jesus will bring justice to a world that has rarely seen it.

Many fantastic things are going to happen, but as with so many aspects of the end times, there are portions of the grand picture we can't understand. The biblical passages are informative but not exhaustive. As a result, Christians have adopted a variety of views on the precise timing of it all.

You'll recall from chapter seven the three views Christians hold about the timing of the rapture. Perhaps it should come as no surprise that Christians also hold three differing views on the timing of the millennium: pre-millennialism, post-millennialism, and a-millennialism. Let's examine these views.

Pre-Millennialism (Pre-Mil)

Pre-millennialists believe that Jesus will return to Earth to reign for a thousand years *before* the last judgment. This view is based on a literal interpretation of Revelation 19–21. Revelation 19 tells us that Jesus Christ will come in power as King of kings and Lord of lords. He will come in judgment and "tread the winepress of the fury of the wrath of God the Almighty" (Revelation 19:15 ESV).

According to the pre-millennial view, by that time, this earth will have already come through the tribulation. Jesus Christ will judge the Antichrist and the false prophet. Then Jesus will bind Satan for a thousand years, so that he can deceive the nations no more. Finally, Jesus will usher in the millennium, when he will rule this world with his resurrected saints.

Now, just to make things really confusing, there are three slightly different views within pre-millennialism; the thing that separates them is the role of the church. Under our view, the church of Jesus Christ will have already been taken to the heavenly Jerusalem by the time the millennium starts. The second view holds that the church will be on Earth during the millennium. And a smaller group of believers argues for a combination of these views, in which the church will be able to go back and forth between heaven and earth during this thousand-year reign.

Post-Millennialism (Post-Mil)

This view teaches that Jesus Christ won't come again until *after* the millennium. Post-millennialists believe we're already in the millennium. Of course that means they have to redefine *millennium*. They believe the millennium is the reign of Christ over the earth through the church. In other words, the millennial reign of Christ is summed up by Christendom, a historical period that began with Roman Emperor Constantine legalizing Christianity and setting the stage for Christianity's powerful influence throughout Europe and other parts of the world.

This view holds that when Christianity spreads the gospel throughout the world and defeats the forces of Satan, Jesus will return to the earth. In this case, everything would already be set up for his reign. For me, this view does not work, in part, because Christendom hasn't successfully produced justice on the earth. In fact, many times Christians have been guilty of some great, historic failures that have instead led to injustice and terror in the earth. The ranks of post-millennialists shrank during the twentieth century, a time of unprecedented war and death and destruction.

A-Millennialism (A-Mil)

A-millennialists believe in a millennium, but they view the word *thousand* differently, saying it is a symbol of completion and wholeness. As they see it, we should think of the millennium as the time between the day of Pentecost (when the church was founded in the book of Acts) and the second coming (when the church will be joined with Christ in the New Jerusalem). In other words, the current church age is the millennium, and Christ is reigning spiritually over the church, not the world. At the end of the church age, Christ's second coming will result in a final judgment for unbelievers and the establishment of a permanent physical reign over the whole world.

Summing Up the Three Millennial Views

Many books have been written on these various systems for understanding the millennium. I'm persuaded that one of the three views we've just discussed makes more sense out of the biblical passages than the other two views.

When we examined the three main Christian approaches to the tribulation (chapter seven), I concluded by saying I couldn't really determine which one best fits the biblical material. That's not the case here. In the case of the millennium, I think the arguments in favor of the pre-millennial view are fairly strong. In part, that's because the other two views take serious liberties with the end time chronologies presented in Revelation 19–21 and in countless Old Testament passages that describe the period following the return of the Messiah as a period of semiperfection and restoration of Israel.

Differences over this issue are not worth fighting over or worth dividing the church over, though such battles have happened many times in the past. Each of us is responsible for choosing a position we think makes the most sense out of the majority of the biblical evidence. I think the Bible speaks clearly on the issue of the millennium and guides Christians to a pre-millennial view that has Christ reigning over the earth *before* the last judgment. But I will continue to embrace and worship with Christians who differ with me on this, including some in my own congregation.

Toward a New Heaven and a New Earth

Debates about the timing of the millennium are human-centered and earth-bound. They're all about us and what will happen to our planet at the end of the age. That's certainly understandable, but I believe God wants us to lift our eyes and our hearts to see beyond our individual concerns. I believe he wants us to grasp something of his cosmic plan for all of creation. In fact, God is going to create a new universe, and he wants us to joyfully anticipate its arrival.

The Bible refers to three heavens. The highest or third heaven is the dwelling place of God. The second heaven is the galactic systems of the cosmos and outer space. And the first heaven is the atmosphere of Earth.

At the dawning of the new heavens and the new earth, these three heavens will become one. At that point, heaven will encompass all the works of God's hand. That's an overwhelming concept, but it shows how big God is and how grand his plans are for the end of the age.

In recent years, astronomers debated whether Pluto was a real planet or just a dwarf planet—that's because science has advanced since many of us studied the planets in school. According to the latest information I've read, the closest star to Earth is Proxima Centauri, which is 4.22 light years away. You could travel there if you could locate a spacecraft capable of traveling 25,000 miles an hour (which is forty times the speed of sound) *and* you had 113,000 years to get there, because that's how long it would take (S. V. Date, "Why the Sky Is the Limit," *Palm Beach Post*, Sep 18, 2005).

I believe that traveling to such places will be part of what we can all do when God institutes his new heaven and new earth. You may say I've been watching too many episodes of *Star Trek,* and that may be true. But I'm also trying to let my mind grasp the amazing things God has planned for us at the end of the age.

Psalm 19 tells us "the heavens are telling the glory of God." Have you ever looked into the night sky and marveled at the handiwork of our Creator? Even this beauty is merely a preview of the glories we'll see after this world has been renewed and restored.

And there's more. At the end of the age, we'll see God face to face, in all of his awesome glory and he will bless us in ways we can't imagine. We'll have resurrection bodies. Thinking about this sends chills up and down my spine. That's why Paul said in Philippians 1, "For me to live is Christ, and to die is gain," because heaven awaits.

Friends, there is so much I don't know about what lies ahead, but it's what I *do* know that moves me to draw closer to God with each breath I take. I'm looking into the future, and, even though I can't see everything clearly, the things I can see are beyond description. I hope you can glimpse these things now and enjoy them with all of God's children for all eternity.

"I Can Only Imagine"—It's a Heavenly Hit

Does a songwriter know when he's writing a classic? Bart Millard of the Christian band MercyMe had no idea the song he wrote in memory of his father would become one of the most popular contemporary Christian songs of all time.

The lyrics are relatively simple and straightforward: "I can only imagine what it will be like when I walk by your side." But the emotions stirred by this song are far from simple. Recorded on the band's 2001 debut album *Almost There*, the song was number one on Christian radio for the year and was sung by Christians in many churches. It earned three Dove Awards in 2002 and was later recorded by Amy Grant and Wynona Judd.

Millard explained the inspiration for his songwriting to a writer for the website FamilyChristian.com.

> It's more or less life experience. I don't know if it's fortunately or unfortunately, going through a lot of different things in life, tragically or good times or whatever. My father passed away of cancer when I was eighteen and I realized a lot of students, more than I thought, could relate. It's not really about having all the answers. It's sharing your feelings. You have two choices when tragic stuff happens. You either run from God or hang on to Him with both hands, and fortunately I found myself hanging on more and more, and through all this finding a more passionate love for Christ.

I hope our discussion of the new heaven and the new earth will inspire you to hang on to God with both hands as we await the glorious future he has for those who love him.

— 10 —

CONCLUSION:

KEEPING THE MAIN THING THE MAIN THING

One of the most important Christian books of all time is C. S. Lewis's *Mere Christianity*. In the preface to that wonderful book, Lewis wrote, "I offer no help to anyone who is hesitating between two Christian 'denominations.' You will not learn from me whether you ought to become an Anglican, a Methodist, a Presbyterian, or a Roman Catholic."

So, what was Lewis trying to accomplish in that book? He explained, "Ever since I became a Christian I have thought that the best, perhaps the only, service I could do for my unbelieving neighbors was to explain and defend the belief that has been common to nearly all Christians at all times."

That is Lewis's definition of "mere" Christianity: "the belief that has been common to nearly all Christians at all times." In a sense, my purpose in this book is to present an overview of "mere" end times—that is, those things Christians believe to be most important about the Last Things.

From the time of Christ, followers of Jesus have needed to agree on core doctrine, including concepts such as human sinfulness, Christ's resurrection from the dead, and the ongoing work of the Holy Spirit. Other core doctrines are described in the Apostles' Creed (see chapter five).

We should not confuse matters of core doctrine with less important issues—such as whether communion should be taken with wine—or with questions the Bible never addresses—such as, Should I vote Republican or Democrat in the next election?

By keeping the main thing the main thing, we can avoid getting sidetracked or confused and starting fights over things about which Christians can legitimately agree to disagree.

The same goes for our discussion of the Last Things. We may disagree about exactly *when* Christ is returning to the earth, precisely *how long* he will be here, and exactly *who* will be here when he arrives.

But there's no disagreeing about the core teachings that came through loud and clear in the many passages examined in this book, including these:

- Conflicts will erupt on the earth as we approach the end times.
- These conflicts in the earthly realm reflect conflicts in the spiritual realm that have endured since the beginning of time.
- The conflicts reflect the opposition between good and evil, heaven and hell, Christ and Satan.
- We should live aware of these conflicts, constantly checking which side we are on.

I've tried in this book to focus on the key things and let the less important things fall by the wayside. Other books may go deeper into one topic or another, and that's fine. But it's important to focus first on the core end-time issues rather than being distracted by side issues that many good scholars disagree on. Paul warned believers not "to occupy themselves with myths and endless genealogies which promote speculations rather than the divine training that is in faith; whereas the aim of our charge is love that issues from a pure heart and a good conscience and sincere faith" (1 Timothy 1:4–5).

Where Do You Stand?

In the introduction, we talked about God wanting us to live in faith, not in fear. We also noted the important difference between rational fears and irrational fears. The fear of being killed tomorrow by a fiery comet is probably an irrational fear. But the nagging fear that you don't know God as you should is perhaps a fear to which you should pay attention.

I accepted Christ when I was five years old as I knelt in the living room with my mom in La Canada, California. With my knees on the floor and my elbows on the sofa, I prayed with her and made a commitment to Christ that was so real I've never forgotten it.

That doesn't mean I've never had doubts. I grew up in a church that had regular revival meetings with guest evangelists. Almost every time an evangelist came to town I would walk down the aisle and recommit myself to the Lord, especially when the evangelist asked that frightful question: "Suppose you walk out of here tonight and are hit by a truck? Where will you spend eternity? With God in heaven, or with Satan in hell?" It got so bad that my dad made me promise not to go forward any more.

It's natural to question our relationship to God. Paul told us to work out our salvation with fear and trembling.

If you've already committed yourself to Christ, then there's no need to fear that your commitment is faulty. But if you have never committed your life to Christ, there's no better time than now to do so.

You can begin by praying this simple prayer.

> Lord Jesus, thank you for dying on the cross for me and paying the penalty for my sin. I ask you to come into my life, please, and forgive me of my sin. Wash me whiter than snow. Cleanse me. And grant me eternal life. I ask you to be my Savior and my Lord. I ask you to sit on the throne of my life from this day forth. And I will seek to follow you and live for you all the days of my life. Amen.

He Is Coming Soon

The Bible records many of Jesus' words, but it saves these five powerful words until the last chapter of Revelation: "Yes, I am coming soon."

Jesus delivered those words about two thousand years ago. Since that time, people who love him and serve him have been waiting for the fulfillment of those words.

I, too, am waiting for the fulfillment of this promise. I'm not sure when it will happen, but I know it will happen some day. I hope to witness these things during my earthly life, but if not, I will be present in the spirit for God's final roll call.

What about you? Do you have a sense of the coming dawn of the Last Things? Some people live in continual fear that the world will, any minute, come crashing down around their heads. Others totally ignore the end times, concluding that there's nothing of relevance for them in these matters.

I believe both positions are in error. Just as we live in a time that's between the creation and the fulfillment of all things, so we must also live in the tension between anticipation and fulfillment.

Nobody knows what Jesus meant by the word *soon*, though many writers have tried to figure out the mind of God. If this book has shown anything, I hope it has shown how important it is to focus on what we're going to do in the time before he comes.

Our lives will last only so long, and the same can be said of our planet. What will we do in the time we have left?

Some people want to store up riches and possessions, but don't we have enough things already? Why not store up for ourselves the kinds of good deeds that will shine throughout eternity?

Some people want to pursue power and glory. But don't we have enough attention already? Wouldn't it be better to spend the time we have left to draw people's attention to God so they will also come to know him and love him?

Some people want to live lives of ease and comfort, but that's not the pattern Jesus gave when he left the safety of heaven to make his home among sinners. If we've achieved comfort in life, perhaps it's time to step out of our comfort zone to bring the blessings of God to others who are not so fortunate.

Whatever God has called each of us to do, whatever wonderful things he has in store, I pray that the words in this book help fulfill that calling with wisdom, peace, and love for all the people in the world Jesus wants to reach through us.